The Constitution of the United States

JAMES M. BECK

TABLE OF CONTENTS

MOTTO

"Where there is no vision, the people perish; but he that keepeth the Law, happy is he."
—Proverbs xxix. 18
"Remove not the ancient landmark, which thy fathers have set."
—Proverbs xxii. 28

DEDICATION

TO THE HON. HARRY M. DAUGHERTY ATTORNEY-GENERAL
OF THE UNITED STATES
A TRUE AND LOYAL FRIEND, A FAIR AND CHIVALROUS FOE
With whom it is the author's great privilege to collaborate as Solicitor-
General in defending and vindicating in the Supreme Court of the United
States the principles and mandates of its Constitution
Chamonix,
July 14 1922

PREFACE

Preface by the Earl of Balfour[1]
I have been greatly honoured by your invitation to take the chair on this interesting occasion. It gives me special pleasure to be able to introduce to this distinguished audience my friend, Mr. Beck, Solicitor-General of the United States. It is a great and responsible office; but long before he held it he was known to the English public and to English readers as the author who, perhaps more than any other writer in our language, contributed a statement of the Allied case in the Great War which produced effects far beyond the country in which it was written or the public to which it was first addressed. Mr. Beck approached that great theme in the spirit of a great judge; he marshalled his arguments with the skill of a great advocate, and the combination of these qualities—qualities, highly appreciated everywhere, but nowhere more than in this Hall and among a Gray's Inn audience—has given an epoch-making character to his work. To-day he comes before us in a different character. He is neither judge nor advocate, but historian: and he offers to guide us through one of the most interesting and important enterprises in which our common race has ever been engaged.

The framers of the American Constitution were faced with an entirely new problem, so far, at all events, as the English-speaking world was concerned; and though they founded their doctrines upon the English traditions of law and liberty, they had to deal with circumstances which none of their British progenitors had to face, and they showed a masterly spirit in adapting the ideas of which they were the heirs to a new country and new conditions. The result is one of the greatest pieces of constructive statesmanship ever accomplished. We, who belong to the British Empire, are at this moment engaged, under very different circumstances, in welding slowly and gradually the scattered fragments of the British Empire into an organic whole, which must, from the very nature of its geographical situation, have a Constitution as different from that of the British Isles, as the Constitution of the British Isles is different from that of the American States. But all three spring from one root; all three are carried out by men of like political ideals; all three are destined to promote the cause of ordered liberty throughout the world. In the meanwhile we on this side of the Atlantic cannot do better than study, under the most favourable and fortunate conditions, the story of the great constitutional adventure which has given us the United States of America.

A.J.B.

[Footnote 1: [Address of the Earl of Balfour as Chairman on the occasion of the delivery on June 13, 1922, in Gray's Inn of the first of the lectures herein reprinted.]

INTRODUCTIONS

INTRODUCTION BY SIR JOHN SIMON, K.C.[2]

I have the privilege and the honour of adding a few words to express our thanks to the Solicitor-General of the United States for this memorable course of lectures. They are memorable alike for their subject and their form; alike for the place in which we are met and for the man who has so generously given of his time and learning for our instruction. Mr. Beck is always a welcome visitor to our shores, and nowhere is he more welcome than in these ancient Inns of Court which are the home and source of law for Americans and Englishmen alike. In contemplating the edifice reared by the Fathers of the American Constitution we take pride in remembering that it was built upon British foundations by men, many of whom were trained in the English Courts; and when Mr. Beck lectures on this subject to us, our interest and our sympathy are redoubled by the thought that whatever differences there may be between the Old World and the New, citizens of the United States and ourselves are the Sons of a Common Mother and jointly inherit the treasure of the Common Law. And we cannot part with Mr. Beck on this occasion without a personal word. Plato records a saying of Socrates that the dog is a true philosopher because philosophy is love of knowledge, and a dog, while growling at strangers, always welcomes the friends that he knows. And the British public often greets its visitors with a touch of this canine philosophy. We regard Mr. Beck, not as a casual visitor, but as a firm friend to whom we owe much; he has been here again and again and we hope will often repeat his visits, and Englishmen will never forget how, at a crisis in our fate, Mr. James Beck profoundly influenced the judgment of the neutral world and vindicated, by his masterly and sympathetic argument, the justice of our cause.

11

[Footnote 2: Address of Sir John Simon on the conclusion, on June 19,1922, of the three lectures herein printed.]

AUTHOR'S INTRODUCTION

This book is a result of three lectures, which were delivered in the Hall of Gray's Inn, London, on June 13, 15, and 19, 1922, respectively, under the auspices and on the invitation of the University of London. The invitation originated with the University of Manchester, which, through its then Vice-Chancellor, Dr. Ramsay Muir, two years ago graciously invited me to visit Manchester and explain American political institutions to the undergraduates. Subsequently I was greatly honoured when the Universities of Cambridge, Edinburgh and London joined in the invitation.

Unfortunately for me—for I greatly valued the privilege of explaining the institutions of my country to the undergraduates of these great Universities—my political duties made it impossible for me to visit England prior to June 1, about which time the Supreme Court of the United States, in which my official duties largely preoccupy my time, adjourns for the summer. Any dates after June 1 were inconvenient to the first three Universities, but it was my good fortune that the University of London was able to carry out the plan, and that it had the cordial co-operation of that venerable Inn of Court, Gray's Inn, one of the "noblest nurseries of legal training."

Thus I was privileged to address at once an academic and a professional audience.

I came to England for this purpose as a labour of love. I had no anticipation of success, for I feared that the interest in the subject-matter of my lectures would be very slight.

My surprise and gratification increased on the occasion of each lecture, as the audiences grew in numbers and distinction. Many leading jurists and statesmen took more than a mere complimentary interest, and some of them, although pressed with social and public duties, honoured me with their attendance at all three lectures. How can I adequately express my appreciation of the great honour thus done me by the Earl of Balfour, the Lord Chancellor, Lord Justice Atkin, the Vice-Chancellor of the University of London, and many other leaders in academic and legal circles—not to forget the Chief Justice of the United States, who paid me the great compliment of attending the last lecture. To one and nil of my auditors, my heartfelt thanks!

I also must not fail to acknowledge the generous space given in the British Press to these lectures, and the even more generous allusions to them in the editorial columns. An especial acknowledgment is due to Viscount

Burnham and The Daily Telegraph for their generous interest in this book. The good cause of Anglo-American friendship has no better friend than Lord Burnham.

This experience has convinced me that now, more than ever before, there is in England a deep interest in American institutions and their history. This is as it should be, for—for better or worse—England and America will play together a great part in the future history of the world. In double harness they are destined to pull the heavy load of the world's problems. Therefore these "yoke-fellows in equity" must know each other better, and, what is more, pull together.

As I was revising the proofs of these lectures in beautiful Chamonix, the prospectus of the Scottish-American Association reached me, in which its Honorary Secretary and my good friend, Dr. Charles Sarolea, took occasion to make the following suggestion to his British compatriots:

"To remove those causes of estrangement, to avoid a fateful catastrophe, in other words, to bring about a cordial understanding with America, the first condition must be an understanding of America. Such an understanding, or even the atmosphere in which such an understanding may grow, has still to be created. It is indeed passing strange that in these days of cheap books and free education, America should be almost a 'terra incognita,' that we should know next to nothing of American history, of the American Constitution, of American practical politics, of the American mentality. We scarcely read American newspapers or American books. Even such masters of classical prose as Francis Parkman, perhaps the greatest historian who has used the English language as his vehicle, are almost unknown to the average reader. Our students do not visit American universities as they used before the War to visit German universities. The consequence is that again and again we are running the risk of perpetrating the most grotesque errors of judgment, of committing the most serious political blunders, in defiance of American public opinion."

The success of my Gray's Inn lectures convinces me that Dr. Sarolea underestimates the interest in America and its history in England. However, the episode, which is treated in these lectures, is, as he says, "terra incognita" not only in England, but even in the United States. It is amazing how little is known in America of the facts given in my second lecture. The American student, after rejoicing in the victory at Yorktown and the end of the War of Independence, generally skips about eight years to 1789, mid his interest in the history of his own country recommences with the inauguration of President Washington.

Students of history in both countries thus miss one of the most interesting and instructive chapters of American history, and indeed of any history.

I have ventured to add to my Gray's Inn lectures another address, which I delivered as the "annual address" at the session of the American Bar Association in Cincinnati, Ohio, on August 31, 1921. I do so, because it has a direct bearing on the decay of the spirit of constitutionalism both in America and elsewhere. It discusses a great malaise of our age, for which, I fear, no written Constitution, however wise, is an adequate remedy. It was published in condensed form in the issue of the Fortnightly for October, 1921, and an acknowledgment is due to its courteous editor for permission to republish it.

I have forborne in these lectures to make more than a passing reference to the League of Nations and the great Conference which framed it, tempting as the obvious analogy was. The reader who studies the appendices will see that the Covenant of the League more nearly resembles the Articles of Confederation than the Constitution of 1787.

I only mention the subject to suggest that the reader of these lectures will better understand why the American people take the written obligations of the League so seriously and literally. We have been trained for nearly a century and a half to measure the validity and obligations of laws and executive acts in Courts of Justice and to apply the plain import of the Constitution. Our constant inquiry is, "Is it so nominated" in that compact? In Europe, and especially England, constitutionalism is largely a spirit of great objectives and ideals.

Therefore, while in these nations the literal obligations of Articles X, XI, XV, and XVI of the Covenant of the League are not taken rigidly, we in America, pursuant to our life-long habit of constitutionalism, interpret these clauses as we do those of our Constitution, and we ask ourselves, Are we ready to promise to do, that which these Articles literally import, join, for example, in a commercial, social and even military war against any nation that is deemed an aggressor, however remote the cause of the war may be to us? Are we prepared to say that in the event of a war or threatened danger of war, the Supreme Council of the League may take any action it deems wise and effectual to maintain peace? This is a very serious committal. Other nations may not take it so literally, but with our life-long adherence to a written Constitution as a solemn contractual obligation, we do.

This is said in no spirit of hostility to the League, but only to explain the American point of view. Since I delivered these lectures, I took a short trip to the Continent, and while sojourning in Geneva, made a visit to the offices of the League. All I there saw greatly interested me, and I could have nothing but a feeling of admiration for the effective and useful administrative work which the League is doing.

The men who framed the Covenant of the League tried to do, under more difficult, but not dissimilar, conditions, what the framers of the American

Constitution did in 1787. In both cases the aim was high, the great purpose meritorious. Those Americans who, for the reasons stated, are not in sympathy with the structural form and political objectives of the League, are not lacking in sympathy for its admirable administrative work in co-ordinating the activities of civilized nations for the common good. In any study of a World Constitution, the example of those who framed the American Constitution can be studied with profit.

JAMES M. BECK.

Chamonix,

July 14, 1922.

THE GENESIS OF THE CONSTITUTION OF THE UNITED STATES

I trust I need not offer this audience, gathered in the noble hall of this historic Inn—of "old Purpulei, Britain's ornament"—any apology for challenging its attention in this and two succeeding addresses to the genesis, formulation, and the fundamental political philosophy of the Constitution of the United States. The occasion gives me peculiar satisfaction, not only in the opportunity to thank my fellow Benchers of the Inn for their graciousness in granting the use of this noble Hall for this purpose, but also because the delivery of these addresses now enables me to be, for the moment, in fact as in honorary title a Bencher, or Reader, of this time-honoured society.

If I needed any justification for addresses, which I was graciously invited to deliver under the auspices of the University of London, an honour which I also gratefully acknowledge, it would lie in the fact that we are to consider one of the supremely great achievements of the English-speaking race. It is in that aspect that I shall treat my theme; for, as a philosophical or juristic discussion of the American Constitution, my addresses will be neither as "deep as a well, nor as wide as a church door."

My auditors will bear in mind that I must limit each address to the duration of an hour, and that I cannot go deeply or exhaustively into a subject that has challenged the admiring comment and profound consideration of the intellectual world for nearly a century and a half.

If England and America are to act together in the coming time—and the destinies of the world are, to a very large extent, in their keeping, then they must know each other better, and, to this end, they must take a greater interest in each other's history and political institutions. My principal purpose in these lectures is to deepen the interest of this great nation in one of the very greatest and far-reaching achievements of our common race.

Americans have never lacked interest in English history; for however broad the stream of our national life, how could we ignore its chief source?

But is there in England an equal interest in the history of America, whose origin and development constitute one of the most dramatic and significant dramas ever played upon the stage of this "wide and universal theatre of man"? It is true that Thackeray, in his Virginians, gave us in fiction the finest picture of our colonial life, and the late and deeply lamented Lord Bryce wrote one of the best commentaries upon our institutions in The American Commonwealth. In more recent years two of the most moving portraits of our Hamilton and Lincoln are due to your Mr. Oliver and Lord Charnwood. We gratefully recognize this; and yet, how many educated Englishmen have studied that little known chapter of our history, which gave to the progress of mankind a contribution to political science which your Gladstone praised as the greatest "ever struck off at a given time by the brain and purpose of man"? If "peace hath her victories no less renown'd than war," this achievement may well justify your study and awaken your admiration; for, as I have already said and cannot too strongly emphasize, it was the work of the English-speaking race, of men who, shortly before they entered upon this great work of constructive statecraft, were citizens of your Empire. The conditions of colonial development had profoundly stimulated in these English pioneers the sense and genius for constitutionalism.

In his speech on Conciliation with America of March 22, 1775, Edmund Burke showed his characteristically philosophic comprehension of this powerful constitutional conscience of the then American subjects of the Empire. After stating that in no other country in the world was law so generally studied, and referring to the fact that as many copies of Blackstone's Commentaries had been sold in America as in England, he added:

"This study renders men acute, inquisitive, dexterous, prompt in attack, ready in defence, full of resources. In other countries the people, more simple and of a less mercurial cast, judge of an ill principle in government only by an actual grievance; here they anticipate the evil, and judge of the pressure of the grievance by the badness of the principle."

Moreover, these hardy pioneers were the privileged heirs of the great political traditions of England. While the Constitution of the United States was very much more than an adaptation of the British Constitution, yet its underlying spirit was that of the English speaking race and the Common Law. Behind the framers of the Constitution, as they entered upon their momentous task, were the mighty shades of Simon de Montfort, Coke, Sandys, Bacon, Eliot, Hampden, Lilburne, Milton, Shaftesbury and Locke.

Could there be a better illustration of Sir Frederick Pollock's noble tribute to the genius of the common law:
"Remember that Our Lady, the Common Law, is not a task-mistress, but a bountiful sovereign, whose service is freedom. The destinies of the English-speaking world are bound up with her fortunes and migrations and its conquests are justified by her works"?

Another reason makes the consideration of the subject not only interesting but opportune. "These are the times that try men's souls." It is a time of sifting, when men of all nations in civilization in these critical days are again testing the value even of those political institutions which have the sanction of the past. Society is in a state of flux. Everywhere the foundations of governmental structures seem to be settling—let us hope and pray upon a surer foundation—and when the seismic convulsion of the world war is taken into account, it is not surprising that this is so. While the storm is not yet past and the waves have not wholly subsided, it is natural that everywhere thoughtful men as true mariners are taking their reckonings to know where they are and whether the frail bark of human institutions is still sufficiently seaworthy to keep afloat.

Moreover, the patent evidences of weakness in the international organization that we call civilization, the imperative need of ending the spirit of moral anarchy, and the urgent necessity of rebuilding the shattered ruins of the social edifice on surer foundations by the integration of the nations, if possible, into some new form of world organization, gives peculiar interest in these terrible days to the manner in which the American people solved a similar problem more than a century ago.

Then, as now, a world war had ended. Then, as now, half the world was prostrated by the wounds of fratricidal strife. As Washington said: "The whole world was in an uproar," and he added that the task "was to steer safely between Scylla and Charybdis." The problem, then as now, was not only to make "the world safe for democracy," but to make democracy, for which there is no alternative, safe for the world. The thirteen colonies in 1787, while small and relatively unimportant, were, however, a little world in themselves, and, relatively to their numbers and resources, this problem, which they confronted and solved, differed in degree but not in kind from that which now confronts civilization. Impoverished in resources, exhausted by the loss of the flower of their youth, demoralized by the reaction from feverish strife, the forces of disintegration had set in in the United States between 1783 and 1787. Law and order had almost perished and the provisional government had been reduced to impotence. A few wise and noble spirits, true Faithfuls and Great Hearts, led a despondent people out of the Slough of Despond till their feet were again on firm ground and their faces turned towards the Delectable Mountains of peace, justice, and liberty. Let it be emphasized that they did this, not by seeking more power, but by imposing restraints upon themselves. That spirit of self-restraint is the essence of the American Constitution.

So enduring was their achievement that to-day the Constitution of the United States is the oldest comprehensive written form of government now existing in the world. Few, if any, forms of government have better withstood the mad spirit of innovation, or more effectively proved their merit by the "arduous greatness of things done."

For this reason, as the nations of the world are now trying in a cosmic form and under similar conditions to do that which the founders of the American Republic in 1787 did in a microcosmic form, a short narration of that earlier achievement may not be unprofitable in this day and generation, when we are blindly groping towards some common basis for international co-ordination.

One of England's greatest Prime Ministers, William Pitt, shortly after the adoption of the Constitution, prophetically said that it would be the admiration of the future ages and the pattern for future constitution building. Time has verified his prediction, for constitution making has been, since the American Constitution was adopted, a continuous industry. The American Constitution has been the classic model for the federated State. Lieber estimated that three hundred and fifty constitutions were made in the first sixty years of the nineteenth century, and, in the constituent States of the American Union, one hundred and three new Constitutions were promulgated in the first century of the United States.

"Have you a copy of the French Constitution?" was asked of a bookseller during the second French Empire, and the characteristically witty Gallic reply was: "We do not deal in periodical literature."

Constitutions, as governmental panaceas, have come and gone; but it can be said of the American Constitution, paraphrasing the noble tribute of Dr. Johnson to the immortal fame of Shakespeare, that the stream of time, which has washed away the dissoluble fabric of many other paper constitutions has left almost untouched its adamantine strength. Excepting the first ten amendments, which were virtually a part of the original charter, only nine others have been adopted in more than one hundred and thirty years.

A constitution, while primarily for the distribution of governmental powers, is, in its last analysis, a formal expression of adherence to that which in modern times has been called the higher law, and which in ancient times was called natural law. The jurisprudence of every nation has, with more or less clearness, recognized the existence of certain primal and fundamental laws which are superior to the laws, statutes, or conventions of living generations. The original use of the term was to import the superiority of the Imperial edict to the laws of the Comitia. All nations have recognized this higher law to a greater or less extent. If we turn to the writings of the most intellectual race in ancient time and possibly in recorded history—the Greeks—we shall see the higher law vindicated with incomparable power in the moral philosophy of its three greatest dramatists, Aeschylus, Sophocles, and Euripides. How was it better expressed than by Antigone when she was asked whether she had transgressed the laws of the state and replied: "Yes, for that law was not from Zeus, nor did Justice, dweller with the gods below, establish it among men; nor deemed I that thy decree—mere mortal that thou art—could override those unwritten and unfailing mandates, which are not of to-day or yesterday, but ever live and no one knows their birthtide."

Five centuries later the greatest of the Roman lawyers and orators, Cicero, spoke in the same terms of a higher law, "which was never written and which we are never taught, which we never team by reading, but which was drawn by nature herself."

The Roman jurists gave it express recognition. They always recognized the distinction between jus civile, or the law of the State, and the jus naturale, or the law of Nature. They nobly conceived that human society was a single unit and that it was governed by a law that was both antecedent and paramount to the law of Rome. Thus, the idea of a higher law transcending the power of a living generation, and therefore eternal as justice itself—became lodged in our system of jurisprudence. Nor was the Common Law wanting in a recognition of a higher law that would curb the power of King or Parliament, for its earlier masters, including four Chief Justices (Coke, Hobart, Holt, and Popham), supported the doctrine, as laid down by Coke, that the judiciary had the power to nullify a law if it were "against common right and reason."—(Bonham's Case, 8 Coke Reports, 114.)

This view as to the limitation of government and the denial of its omnipotence was powerfully accentuated in America by the very conditions of its colonization. The good yeomen of England who journeyed to America went in the spirit of the noble and intrepid Kent, when, turning his back upon King Lear's temporary injustice, he said that he would "shape his old course in a country new." Was it strange that the early colonists, as they braved the hardships and perils of a dangerous voyage, only to be confronted in the wilderness by disease, famine and massacre, should fall back for their own government upon these primal verities of human society, and claim not only their inherited rights as Englishmen, but also the peculiar privileges of pioneers in an unconquered wilderness?

This spirit of constitutionalism in America, which culminated in the Constitution of the United States, had its institutional origin in the spacious days of Queen Elizabeth. That wonderful age, which gave to the world not only Shakespeare, Spenser and Jonson, but also Drake, Frobisher and Raleigh, was the Anglo-Saxon reaction to the Renaissance. The spirit of man had a new birth and was breaking away from the too rigid bonds of ancient custom and authority.

Among the notable, but little known, leaders of that time was Sir Edwin Sandys, the leading spirit of the London (or Virginia) company. He was a Liberal when to be such was an "extra hazardous risk." He was the son of a Liberal, for his father, a great prelate, had been sent to the Tower for preaching in defence of Lady Jane Grey. The son, Sir Edwin, was the foe of monopolies, and in the same Parliament that impeached the great genius of this Inn, Francis Bacon, Sandys advocated the then novel proposition that accused prisoners should have the right to be represented by counsel, to which the strange objection was made that it would subvert the administration of justice. As early as 1613, he had boldly declared in Parliament that even the King's authority rested upon the clear understanding that there were reciprocal conditions which neither ruler nor subject could violate with impunity. He might not too fancifully be called the "Father of American Constitutionalism," for he caused a constitution—possibly the first time that that word was ever applied to a comprehensive scheme of government—to be drafted for the little colony of Virginia in 1609 and amplified in 1612. Speaking in this venerable Hall, whose very walls eloquently remind us of the mighty genius of Francis Bacon, it is interesting to recall that these two charters of government, which were the beginning of Constitutionalism in America and therefore the germ of the Constitution of the United States, were put in legal form for royal approval by Lord Bacon himself. Thus the immortal Treasurer of this Inn is directly linked with the development of Constitutional freedom in America.

Bacon became a member of the council for the Virginia Company in 1609. His deep interest in it is attested in the dedication to him by William Strachey in 1618 of the latter's Historie of Travaile into Virginia Brittania.

In his speech in the House of Commons on January 30, 1621, Bacon saw a vision of the future and predicted the growth of America, when he said:

"This kingdom now first in His Majesty's Times hath gotten a lot or portion in the New World by the plantation of Virginia and the Summer Islands. And certainly it is with the kingdoms on earth as it is in the kingdom of heaven, sometimes a grain of mustard seed proves a great tree."

Truly the mustard seed of Virginia did become a great tree in the American Commonwealth.

One of Bacon's nephews, also of the Inns of Court, Nathaniel Bacon, became the first Liberal leader in the Colonies, and led the first revolt against colonial misrule. He was probably of Gray's Inn, for it is difficult to imagine a Bacon studying in any Inn than the one to which the great Bacon had given so much loving care.

Due to these charters, on July 30, 1619, the little remnant of colonists whom disease and famine had left untouched were summoned to meet in the church at Jamestown to form the first parliamentary assembly in America, the first-born of the fruitful Mother of Parliaments. It was due to Sandys not only that the first permanent English settlement in the Western World was planted at Jamestown in 1607, but that a later group of "adventurers"—for such they called themselves—destined to be more famous, were driven by chance of wind and wave to land on the coast of Massachusetts. Thus was established, not only the beginning of England's colonial Empire—still one of the most beneficent forces in the world—but also the principle of local self-government, which, in the Western World, was destined to develop the American Commonwealth. The compact, signed in the cabin of the Mayflower, while not in strictness a constitution, like the Virginia Charter, was yet destined to be a landmark of history.

Sandys suffered for his convictions, for the party of reaction convinced King James that Virginia was a nest of sedition, and the arbitrary ruler, in the reorganization of the London company, gave a pointed admonition by saying: "Choose the devil, if you will, but not Sir Edwin Sandys." In 1621 he was committed to the Tower and only released after the House of Commons had made a vigorous protest against his incarceration. His successor as treasurer of the London company was Shakespeare's patron, the Earl of Southampton, and it is not a fanciful conjecture to assume that, when the news of the disaster which befell one of the fleets of the London Company on the Island of Bermuda reached England, it inspired Shakespeare to write his incomparable sea idyl, The Tempest. If so, this lovely drama was Shakespeare's unconscious apostrophe to America, for in Ariel—seeking to be free—can be symbolized her awakening spirit, while Prospero, with his thaumaturgic achievements, suggests a constructive genius, which in a little more than a century has made one of the least of the nations to-day one of the greatest.

Bacon, Sandys, Southampton and the Liberal leaders of the House of Commons had implanted in the ideas of the colonists the spirit of constitutionalism, which was destined to influence profoundly the whole development of the American colonies, and finally to culminate in the Constitution of the United States.

The later struggle in the Long Parliament, the fall of Charles I, and more especially the deposition of James II, the accession of William of Orange, and the substitution for the Stuart claim of divine right that of the supremacy of the people in Parliament, naturally had their reaction in the Western World in intensifying the spirit of constitutionalism in the growing American Commonwealth.

The colonial history was therefore increasingly marked by a spirit of individualism, a natural partiality for local rule, and a tenacious adherence to their special privileges, whether granted to Crown colonies, like New

Hampshire, New York, New Jersey, Virginia, the two Carolinas, and Georgia, or proprietary governments, like Maryland, Delaware, and Pennsylvania, or charter governments, such as Massachusetts, Rhode Island, and Connecticut. In the three colonies last named formal corporate charters were granted by the Crown, which in themselves were constitutions in embryo, and the colonists thus acquired written rights as to the government of their internal affairs, upon the maintenance of which they jealously insisted. Thus arose the spirit in America, which treated constitutional rights, not so much as special privileges granted by plenary Sovereignty, but as contractual obligations which could be enforced in the Courts against the Sovereign.

All this developed in the colonists a powerful sense of constitutional morality, and its pertinency to my present theme lies in the fact that when each of the thirteen colonies became, at the conclusion of the War of Independence, a separate and independent nation, they were more concerned, in establishing a central government, to limit its authority and to maintain local self-government than they were to give to the new-born nation the powers which it needed. They carried their constitutionalism to extremes, which nearly made a strong and efficient central government an impossibility.

Nothing was less desired by them than a unified government. It was destined to be wrung from their hard necessities. The Constitution was the reflex action of two opposing tendencies, the one the imperative need of an efficient central government, and the other the passionate attachment to local self-rule. Co-operation between the colonies had been a matter of long discussion and earnest debate, and primarily resulted from the necessity of defence against a common foe the French in Canada, and the Indians of the forest. In 1643 four of the New England colonies united in a league to defend themselves. In 1693 William Penn made the first suggestion for a union of all the colonies. In 1734 a council was held at Albany at the instance of the Crown to provide the means for the defence against France in Canada, and it was then that Franklin submitted the first concrete form for a union of the colonies into a permanent alliance. It was in advance of the times, for, conservative as it was, it was unfortunately opposed both by the Crown and the colonies themselves.

The time was not ripe for any such union, and the reason was apparent. The colonies differed very much in the character of their populations, in the nature of their economic interests, and in their political antecedents. They were not wholly of the English race. Many nations in Europe had already contributed to the population. For example, New York was partly Dutch, and in Pennsylvania there was a considerable element of the Swedes, Germans, and Swiss. Moreover, the colonists were as widely separated from each other, measured by the facilities of locomotion, as are the most remote nations of the world to-day. Only a few men ever found occasion to leave their colony to journey to another, and most men never left, from birth to death, the community in which they lived. Outside of the few scattered communities in the different colonies there was an almost unbroken wilderness, with few wagon roads and in places only a bridle path. The only methods of communication were the letters and still fewer newspapers, which were carried by post riders often through an almost trackless wilderness.

Obviously, a working government could not easily be constituted between peoples of different religions, races, and economic interests, who, for the most part, never met each other face to face and with whom frequent communication was impossible.

The differences between the colonies and the mother-country with respect to internal taxation slowly developed into an issue of constitutionalism rather than of legislative policy. As in England, the immediate question affected the power of the Crown to give to the customs inspectors the power to make general searches and seizures, to enforce the navigation laws. In 1761 James Otis, of Massachusetts, made a fateful speech before the colonial legislature, in which, asserting the illegality of the search warrants on the ground that they violated the constitutional rights of Englishmen to protection in their own homes, he asserted that Acts of Parliament which violated the sanctity of the home were void and that, more specifically, they violated the charter granted to Massachusetts. Asserting the doctrine which at that time was the doctrine of the English common law, as stated by Coke and three other Chief Justices, he said:

"To say the parliament is absolute and arbitrary is a contradiction. The Parliament cannot make two and two five. Omnipotency cannot do it.... Parliaments are in all cases to declare what is for the good of the whole; but it is not the declaration of parliament that makes it so: there must be in every instance a higher authority, viz., GOD. Should an Act of Parliament be against any of His natural laws, which are immutably true, their declaration would be contrary to eternal truth, equity and justice, and consequently void; and so it would be adjudged by the Parliament itself, when convinced of their mistake."

It is a curious fact that in the reaction from the tyranny of the Stuarts your country abandoned this principle of the common law by substituting for the omnipotence of the Crown the omnipotence of Parliament, while in my country the somewhat vague and unworkable principle of the common law, which gave the judiciary the power to invalidate an act of the legislature, when against natural reason and justice, was developed into the great principle, without which institutions in an heterogeneous and widely scattered democracy would be unworkable, namely that the powers of government are strictly defined, and that neither the executive, the legislative, nor the judicial departments of the government can go beyond the precise limits established by the fundamental law. Like the common law, the Constitution was thus the result of a slow evolution. Mr. Gladstone, in his oft-quoted remark, gave an erroneous impression when he said:

"As the British Constitution is the most subtle organism which has proceeded from progressive history, so the American Constitution is the most wonderful work ever struck off, at a given time by the brain and purpose of man."

This assumes that the Constitution sprang, like Minerva, armed cap-à-pie, from the brain of the American people, whereas it was as much the result of a slow, laborious, and painful evolution as was the British Constitution. Probably Gladstone so understood the development of the American Constitution and recognized that its framing was only the culmination of an evolution of many years.

When the constitutional struggle between the colonies and the Parliament became acute, the necessity of a union for a common defence became imperative. As early as July, 1773, Franklin recommended the "convening of a General Congress" so that the colonies would act together. His suggestion was introduced in the Virginia House of Burgesses in May, 1774, and as a result there met in Philadelphia on September 5 of that year the first Continental Congress, styled by themselves: "The Delegates appointed by the Good People of these Colonies." Nothing was further from their purpose than to form a central government or to separate from England. This Congress only met as a conference of representatives of the colonies to defend what they conceived to be their constitutional rights.

Before the second Continental Congress met in the following year, the accidental clash at Lexington and Concord had taken place, and as the Congress again re-convened a momentous change had taken place, which was, in fact, the beginning of the American Commonwealth. The Congress became by force of circumstances a provisional government, and as such it might well have claimed plenary powers to meet an immediate exigency. So indisposed were they to separate from England or to substitute for its rule that of a new government, that the Continental Congress, when it then involuntarily took over the government of America, failed to exercise any adequate power. It remained simply a conference without real power. Each colony had one vote and the rule of unanimity prevailed. Even its decisions were largely advisory, for they amounted to little more than recommendations to the constituent States as to what measures should be taken. Each colony complied with the recommendation in its discretion and in its own way. Notwithstanding this fatal lack of authority, the Continental Congress, then actually engaged in civil war, created an army, and, through its committees, entered into negotiations with foreign nations. To support the former, it issued paper money, with the disastrous result that could be readily anticipated. While it had a presiding officer, it had no executive, and the new nation, which was hardly conscious of its own birth, had no judiciary.

Had this de facto government assumed the plenary powers which provisional governments must, under similar circumstances, necessarily assume, it would have been better for the cause of the colonists. For want of an efficient central government, the civil administration of the infant nation was marked by a weakness and incapacity that defeated Washington's plans and nearly broke his spirit. Washington's little army was the victim of the gross incapacity of an impotent government. The soldiers came and went, not as the general commanded, but as the various colonies permitted. The tragedy of Valley Forge, when the little army nearly starved to death, and literally the soldiers could be tracked over the snows by their bleeding, unshod feet, was not due to lack of clothing and provisions, but to the gross incapacity of a headless government that if it had had the wisdom to act lacked the authority. The situation was one of chaos. The colonies recruited their own contingents, paid such taxes as they pleased, which grew increasingly less, and the Congress had no coercive power to enforce its policies, either with reference to internal or external affairs. This situation was so clearly recognized that immediately after the Declaration of Independence on July 4, 1776, the draft of a constitution was proposed to give the central government more effective power; but, although the necessity was manifest and most urgent, the so-called Articles of Confederation, which were then drafted in 1776, were never finally adopted by the requisite number of States until March, 1781, when the war was nearly over. As the result proved, they marked only a very small advance over the existing de facto government, for the constituent States were still too jealous of each other and too hostile to the creation of a central government to form a truly effective government. The founders of the Republic could only learn from their errors, but it is their great merit that they had the ability to profit in the stern school of experience, of which Franklin has said that it is a "dear school, but fools will learn in no other."

The founders of the Republic were not fools, and while they did not, as Gladstone seems to intimate, have the inspired wisdom to develop a wonderful Constitution by sheer intuition unaided by experience, they did have the ability to make of their very errors the stepping-stones to a higher destiny.

By the Articles of Confederation, which, as stated, became effective in 1781, the conduct of foreign affairs was vested in the new government, which was also given the power to create admiralty courts, regulate coinage, maintain an army and navy, borrow money, and emit bills of credit, but the great limitation was that in all other respects the constituent States retained absolute power, especially with reference to commerce and taxation. All that the central government could do was to requisition the States to furnish food supplies, and the States were then left to impose the taxes and, if necessary, to enforce their payment in their own way, with the inevitable result that they vied with each other in the struggle to evade them. The Confederation had no direct power over the citizens of the several States. Moreover, the Congress could not levy any taxes, or indeed pass any measure unless nine out of the thirteen States agreed, and the Constitution could not be amended except by unanimous vote. While the Congress could select a presiding officer to serve for one year, yet he had no real executive authority. During the recess of the Congress, a committee of thirteen, consisting of one delegate from each State, had ad interim powers, but not greater than the Congress, which they represented.

Such a government would have been fatal to any people, and so it nearly proved to be to the infant nation. Two circumstances saved them from the consequences of such incapacity: one was the invaluable aid of France, and the other the personality of George Washington. Of this great leader, one of the noblest that ever "lived in the tide of time," it is only necessary to quote the fine tribute paid to him by the greatest of the Victorian novelists in his Virginians:

"What a constancy, what a magnanimity, what a surprising persistence against fortune!... Washington, the chief of a nation in arms, doing battle with distracted parties; calm in the midst of conspiracy; serene against the open foe before him and the darker enemies at his back; Washington, inspiring order and spirit into troops hungry and in rags; stung by ingratitude, but betraying no anger, and every ready to forgive; in defeat invincible, magnanimous in conquest and never so sublime as on that day when he laid down his victorious sword and sought his noble retirement— here, indeed, is a character to admire and revere; a life without a stain, a fame without a flaw."

A year after the Articles of Confederation had been adopted, the war came to an end by a preliminary treaty on November 30, 1782.

Now follows the least known chapter in American history. It was a period of travail, of which the Constitution of the United States and the present American nation were born. The government slowly succumbed from its own weakness to its inevitable death. Only the shreds and patches of authority were left. Gradually the union fell apart. Of the Continental Congress only fifteen members, representing seven colonies, remained to transact the affairs of the new nation. The army, which previously to the termination of the war had dissolved by the hundreds, was now unpaid and in a stale of revolt. Measure after measure was proposed in Congress to raise money to pay the interest on the bonded indebtedness, which was in arrears, and to provide funds for the most necessary expenses, but these failed, in Congress for the want of the necessary nine votes or, if enacted, the States treated the requisitions with indifference. The currency of the United States had fallen almost as low as the Austrian kronen, and men derisively plastered the walls of their houses with the worthless paper of the Continental Congress. Adequate authority no longer remained to carry out the terms of the treaties with England and France, and they were nullified by the failure of the infant nation to comply with its own obligations and the consequent refusal of the other contracting parties to comply with theirs. The government made a call upon the States to raise $8,000,000 for the most vital needs, but only $400,000 was actually received. Then Congress asked the States to vest in it the power to levy a tax of five per cent, on imports for a limited period, but, after waiting two years for the action of the States, less than nine concurred. The States were then asked to pledge their own internal revenue for twenty-five years to meet the national indebtedness, but this could only be done by unanimous consent, and while twelve States concurred, Rhode Island refused and the measure was defeated. It was again the infinite folly of the liberum veto which, prior to the great partition, condemned Poland to chronic anarchy.

The impotence of the new government, which was still sitting in Philadelphia, can be measured by the fact that on June 9, 1783, word came that eighty soldiers were on their way to Philadelphia to demand relief. They stacked their arms in front of the State House, where the Congress was then sitting, and refused to disband, when requested by Col. Alexander Hamilton, as the representative of the Congress, to do so. When Congress appealed to the government of Pennsylvania for protection, it was advised that the Pennsylvania militia was likewise insubordinate. The Congress then hastily fled by night and became a fugitive.

The impotence of the Confederation can be measured by the fact that in the last fourteen months of its existence its receipts were less than $400,000, while the interest on the foreign debt alone was over $2,400,000, and the interest on the internal debt was five-fold greater.

In the absence of any government and in the period of general prostration it was not unnatural that the spirit of Bolshevism grew with alarming rapidity. It even permeated the officers of the Army. In March, 1783, an anonymous communication was sent to Washington's officers to meet in secret conference to take some action, possibly to overthrow the government. A copy fell into Washington's hands and, while he forbade the assemblage of the officers under the anonymous call, he himself directed the officers to assemble. He unexpectedly appeared at the meeting and, being no speaker, he had reduced his appeal to writing. As he adjusted his spectacles to read it, he pathetically said: "I have not only grown gray but blind in your service." He then made a touching appeal to them not to increase by example the spreading spirit of revolt. The very sight of their old commander turned the hearts of the revolting element and the officers remained loyal to their noble leader.

Where the spirit of disaffection was thus found in high places it naturally prevailed more widely among the masses who had been driven to frenzy by their sufferings. This culminated in a revolt in Massachusetts under the leadership of an old soldier named Shays, and it spread with such rapidity that not only did one-fifth of the people join in attempting to overthrow the remnant of established authority in Massachusetts, but it rapidly spread to other States. The offices of government and the courthouses were seized, the collection of debts was forbidden, and private property was forcibly appropriated to meet the common needs.

Chaos had come again. It filled Washington's heart with disgust and despair. After surrendering his commission to the pitiful remnant of the government he had retired to Mount Vernon, and for a time declined to act further as the leader of his people. Thus, in October, 1785, he wrote James Warren, of Massachusetts:

"The war, as you have very justly observed, has terminated most advantageously for America, and a fair field is presented to our view; but I confess to you freely, my dear sir, that I do not think we possess wisdom or justice enough to cultivate it properly. Illiberality, jealousy, and local policy mix too much in all our public councils for good government of the union. In a word, the Confederation appears to me to be little more than a shadow without the substance, and Congress a nugatory body, their ordinances being little attended to…. By such policy as this the wheels of government are clogged, and our brightest prospects, and that high expectation which was entertained of us by the wondering world, are turned into astonishment; and, from the high ground on which we stood, we are descending into the vale of confusion and darkness."

Again he wrote to George Mason:

"I have seen without despondency, even for a moment, the hours which America has styled its gloomy ones, but I have beheld no day since the commencement of hostilities that I thought our liberties in such imminent danger as at present. Indeed, we are verging so fast to destruction that I am feeling that sense to which I have been a stranger until within these three months."

Again in 1786 he writes:

"I think often of our situation, and view it with concern. From the high ground we stood upon, from the plain path which invited our footsteps, to be so fallen, so lost, is mortifying; but everything of virtue has, in a degree, taken its departure from our land…. What, gracious God, is man that there should be such inconsistency, and perfidiousness in his conduct! It was but the other day that we were shedding our blood to obtain the Constitutions under which we now live, and now we are unsheathing our swords to overturn them. The thing is so unaccountable that I hardly know how to

realize it or to persuade myself that I am not under an illusion of a dream."
It was, however, the darkest hour before the dawn, and again it was Washington who became his country's saviour. In 1785, some commissioners from the States of Virginia and Maryland visited Mount Vernon to pay their respects to the well-loved commander. After conferring with him upon the chaos of the times, they decided to issue a call for a general conference of the representatives of the States to be held on September 11, 1786, at Annapolis, Maryland, to discuss how far the States themselves could agree on common regulations of commerce. At the appointed time the delegates assembled from Virginia, Pennsylvania, Delaware, New York and New Jersey, and finding themselves too few in number to achieve the great objective, the convention contented itself by issuing another call, drafted by Alexander Hamilton, then under thirty years of age, to all the States to send delegates to a convention to be held in Philadelphia on the second Monday in May, 1787, "to take into consideration the situation of the United States, to devise such further provisions as should appear to them necessary to render the Constitution of the Federal Government adequate to the exigencies of the Union."
The dying Congress tardily approved of this suggestion, but finally, on January 21, 1787, grudgingly adopted a resolution that—
"It is expedient that on the second Monday in May next a convention of delegates, who shall have been appointed by the several States, be held at Philadelphia for the sole and express purpose of revising the Articles of Confederation and reporting to Congress and the several legislatures such alterations and provisions therein as shall, when agreed to in Congress and conformed to by the States, render the Federal Constitution adequate to the exigency of the government and the preservation of the union."
It will be noted by the italicized portions of the resolution that this impotent body thus vainly attempted to cling to the shadow of its vanished authority by stating that the proposed constitutional convention should merely revise the worthless Articles of Confederation and that such amendments should not have validity until adopted by Congress as well as by the people of the several States. How this mandate was disregarded and how the convention was formed, and proceeded to create a new government with a new Constitution, and how it achieved its mighty work, will be the subject of the next lecture.
Anticipating the masterly ability with which a seemingly impotent and dying nation plucked from the nettle of danger the flower of safety, let me conclude this first address by quoting the words of de Tocqueville, in his remarkable work Democracy in America, where he says:
"The Federal Government, condemned to impotence by its Constitution and no longer sustained by the presence of common danger ... was already on the verge of destruction when it officially proclaimed its inability to

conduct the government and appealed to the constituent authority of the nation…. It is a novelty in the history of a society to see a calm and scrutinizing eye turned upon itself, when apprised by the legislature that the wheels of government are stopped; to see it carefully examine the extent of the field and patiently wait for two years until a remedy was discovered, which it voluntarily adopted, without having ever wrung a tear or a drop of blood from mankind."

THE GREAT CONVENTION

Now follows a notable and yet little known scene in the drama of history. It reveals a people who, without shedding a drop of blood, calmly and deliberately abolished one government, substituted another, and erected it upon foundations which have hitherto proved enduring. Even the superstructure slowly erected upon these foundations has suffered little change in the most changing period of the world's history, and until recently its additions, few in number, have varied little from the plans of the original architects. The Constitution is to-day, not a ruined Parthenon, but rather as one of those Gothic masterpieces, against which the storms of passionate strife have beaten in vain. The foundations were laid at a time when disorder was rampant and anarchy widely prevalent. As I have already shown in my first lecture, credit was gone, business paralysed, lawlessness triumphant, and not only between class and class, but between State and State, there were acute controversies and an alarming disunity of spirit. To weld thirteen jealous and discordant States, demoralized by an exhausting war, into a unified and efficient nation against their wills, was a seemingly impossible task. Frederick the so-called Great had said that a federal union of widely scattered communities was impossible. Its final accomplishment has blinded the world to the essential difficulty of the problem.

The time was May 25, 1787; the place, the State House in Philadelphia, a little town of not more than 20,000 people, and, at that time, as remote, measured by the facilities of communication, to the centres of civilization as is now Vladivostok.

The dramatis personae in this drama, though few in numbers, were, however, worthy of the task.

Seventy-two had originally been offered or given credentials, for each State was permitted to send as many delegates as it pleased, inasmuch as the

States were to vote in the convention as units. Of these, the greatest actual attendance was fifty-five, and at the end of the convention a saving remnant of only thirty-nine remained to finish a work which was to immortalize its participants.

While this notable group of men contained a few merchants, financiers, farmers, doctors, educators, and soldiers, of the remainder, at least thirty-one were lawyers, and of these many had been justices of the local courts and executive officers of the commonwealths. Four had studied in the Inner Temple, at least five in the Middle Temple, one at Oxford under the tuition of Blackstone and two in Scottish Universities. Few of them were inexperienced in public affairs, for of the original fifty-five members, thirty-nine had been members of the first or second Continental Congresses, and eight had already helped to frame the constitutions of their respective States. At least twenty-two were college graduates, of whom nine were graduates of Princeton, three of Yale, two of Harvard, four of William and Mary, and one each from the Universities of Oxford, Columbia, Glasgow, and Edinburgh. A few already enjoyed world-wide fame, notably Doctor Franklin, possibly the most versatile genius of the eighteenth century and universally known and honoured as a scientist, philosopher, and diplomat, and George Washington, whose fame, even at that day, had filled the world with the noble purity of his character.

It was a convention of comparatively young men, the average age being little above forty. Franklin was the oldest member, being then eighty-one; Dayton, the youngest, being twenty-seven. With the exception of Franklin and Washington, most of the potential personalities in the convention were under forty. Thus, James Madison, who contributed so largely to the plan that he is sometimes called "The Father of the Constitution," was thirty-six. Charles Pinckney, who, unaided, submitted the first concrete draft of the Constitution, was only twenty-nine, and Alexander Hamilton, who was destined to take a leading part in securing its ratification by his powerful oratory and his very able commentaries in the Federalist papers, was only thirty.

Above all they were a group of gentlemen of substance and honour, who could debate for four months during the depressing weather of a hot summer without losing their tempers, except momentarily—and this despite vital differences—and who showed that genius for toleration and reconciliation of conflicting views inspired by a common fidelity to a great objective that is the highest mark of statesmanship. They represented the spirit of representative government at its best in avoiding the cowardice of time-servers and the low cunning of demagogues. All apparently were inspired by a fine spirit of self-effacement. Selfish ambition was conspicuously absent. They differed, at times heatedly, but always as gentlemen of candour and honour. The very secrecy of their deliberations, of which I shall presently speak, is ample proof how indifferent they were to popular applause and the civium ardor prava jubentium.

The convention had been slow in assembling. Ample notice had been given that it would convene on May 13, 1787, but when that day arrived a mere handful of the delegates, less than a quorum, had assembled.

The Virginia delegation, six in number, and forming probably the ablest delegation from any State, arriving in time, and failing to find a quorum then assembled, employed the period of waiting in submitting to the Pennsylvania delegation the outlines of a plan for the new Constitution. The plan was largely the work of James Madison, and how long it had been in preparation cannot be definitely stated. It is clear that four years before a Philadelphia merchant, one Peletiah Webster, had published a brochure proposing a scheme of dual sovereignty, under which the citizens would owe a double allegiance—one to the constituent States within the sphere of their reserved powers, and one to a federated government within the sphere of its delegated powers. Leagues of States had often existed, but a league which, within a prescribed sphere, would have direct authority over the citizens of the constituent States, without, however, abolishing the authority of such States as to their reserved sphere of power, was a novel theory. How far the Virginia project had been influenced by Webster's suggestion is not clear, but it is certain that before the convention met Pennsylvania and Virginia, two of the most powerful States, were committed to it.

The suggestion was a radical one, for the States, with few exceptions, were chiefly insistent upon the preservation of their sovereignty, and while they were willing to amend the Articles of Confederation by giving fuller authority to the central government, such as it was, the suggestion of subordinating the States to a new sovereign power, whose authority within circumscribed limits was to be supreme, was opposed to all their conventions and traditions. Washington, however, had warmly welcomed the creation of a strong central government, and his correspondence with the leading men of the colonies for some years previously had been burdened with arguments to convince them that a mere league of States would not suffice to create a stable nation. To George Washington, soldier and statesman, is due above all men the ideal of a federated union, for without his influence—that of a noble and unselfish leader—the great result would probably never have been secured. While still waiting for the convention, to meet, and while discussing what was expedient and practicable when they did meet, Washington one day said to a group of delegates, who were considering the acute nature of the crisis:

"It is too probable that no plan that we propose will be adopted. Perhaps another dreadful conflict is to be sustained. If, to please the people, we offer what we ourselves disapprove, how can we afterwards defend our work? Let us raise a standard to which the wise and just can repair. The event is in the hand of God."

Noble words, fit to be written in letters of gold over the portal of every legislature of the world, and it was in this spirit that the convention finally convened on May 25th, 1787.

When the delegates from nine States had assembled, Washington was unanimously elected the presiding officer of the convention. It began by adopting rules of order, and the most significant of these was the provision for secrecy. No copy should be taken of any entry on the Journal, or even permission given to inspect it, without leave of the convention, and "nothing spoken in the house be printed or otherwise published or communicated without leave." The yeas and nays should not be recorded. The rule of secrecy was enlarged by an unwritten understanding that, even when the convention had adjourned, no disclosure should be made of its proceedings during the life of its members. When after nearly four months, the convention adjourned, the secret had been kept, and no one knew even the concrete result of its deliberations until the Constitution itself, and nothing else, was offered to the approval of the people. The high-way, upon which the State House fronted, was covered with earth, to deaden the noise of traffic, and sentries were posted at every means of ingress and egress, to prevent any intrusion upon the privacy of the convention. The members were not photographed daily for the pictorial Press, nor did any cinema register their entrance into the simple colonial hall where they were to meet. Notwithstanding this limitation—for no present-day conference or assembly can proceed with its labours until its members are photographed for the curiosity of the public—these simple-minded gentlemen—less intent upon their appearance than their task—were to accomplish a work of enduring importance.

The extreme care which was taken to preserve this secrecy inviolate, and its purpose, were indicated in an incident handed down by tradition.

One of the members dropped a copy of a proposition then before the convention for consideration, and it was found by another of the delegates and handed to General Washington. At the conclusion of the session, Washington arose and sternly reprimanded the member for his carelessness by saying:

"I must entreat gentlemen to be more careful, lest our transactions get into the newspapers and disturb the public repose by premature speculations. I know not whose paper it is, but there it is [throwing it down on the table]. Let him who owns it, take it."

He then bowed, picked up his hat and left the room with such evidences of annoyance that, like school-children, no delegate was willing to admit the ownership of the paper.

The thought suggests itself: How different the result at Versailles and Genoa might have been had there been the same reasonable provisions for discussion and action uninfluenced by too premature public comment of the day! In these days, when representative government has degenerated into government by a fleeting public opinion, the price we pay for such government by, for and of the Press, is too often the inability of representatives to do what they deem wise and just.

At the close of the convention its records were committed into the keeping of Washington, with instructions to "retain the journal and other papers, subject to order of Congress, if ever formed under the Constitution."

Even the journal consisted of little more than daily memoranda, from which the minutes ought to have been, but never were, made; and these fragmentary records of the proceedings of a convention which had been in continuous session for nearly four months were never published until the year 1819, or thirty-two years after the close of the convention. Thus, the American people knew nothing of their greatest convention until a generation later, and then only a few bones of the mastodon were exhibited to their curious gaze.

The members of the convention kept its secrets inviolate for many years. With few exceptions, the great secrets of the convention died with them. Only one, James Madison, left a comprehensive statement of the more formal proceedings. With this notable exception, only a few anecdotes, handed down by tradition, escaped oblivion. The first of the number to break the pledge of secrecy was Robert Yates, Chief Justice of New York, who, in 1821, published his recollections; but, as he had left the convention a few months after it began, his notes ceased with the 5th of July.

The world would thus have been for ever ignorant of the details of one of the most remarkable conventions in the annals of mankind had it not been that one of the ablest of their number, James Madison, regularly attended the sessions and kept notes from day to day of the debates. While he was not a stenographer, he had a gift for condensing a speech and fairly representing its substance. He jealously guarded his Journal of the Convention until his death. Its very existence was known to few. He died in 1836, and four years later the government purchased the manuscript from his widow. Then, for the first time, the curtain was measurably raised upon the proceedings of a convention which had created, as we now know, one of the greatest nations in history. Fifty-three years after the close of the convention, and when nearly every one of its participants were dead, Madison's Journal was first published.

When was a great secret better kept? Grateful as posterity must be for this inestimable gift of great human enterprise, yet even Madison's careful journal fills one with the deepest regret that this wonderful debate, which lasted for nearly four months between men of no ordinary ability, could not have been preserved to the world.

Two or three of the speeches which Madison gives in his Journal are complete, for when Doctor Franklin spoke he reduced his remarks to writing and gave a copy to Madison, but of the other speeches only a fragrant remains. Thus, that "admirable Crichton," Alexander Hamilton, addressed the convention in a speech that lasted five hours, in which he stated his philosophy of government, but of that only a short condensation, and possibly not even an accurate fragment, remains.

Without this extraordinary provision for secrecy, which is so opposed to modern democratic conventions, and which so little resembles the famous point as to "open covenants openly arrived at," the convention could not have accomplished its great work, for these wise men realized that a statesman cannot act wisely under the observation of a gallery, and especially when the gallery compels him by the pressure of public opinion to work as it directs. I recognize that public opinion—often temporarily uninformed but in the end generally right—does often save the democracies of the world from the selfish ends of self-seeking and misguided leadership; but, given noble and wise representatives, they work best when least influenced by the fleeting passions of the day.

It is evident that if the framers of the Constitution had met, as similar conventions have within recent years met at Versailles and Genoa, with the world as their gallery and with the representatives of the Press as an integral part of the conference, they would have accomplished nothing. The probability is that the convention would not have lasted a month if their immediate purpose had been to placate current opinion. It may be doubted whether such a convention, if called to-day, either in your country or mine, could achieve like results, for in this day of unlimited publicity, when men divide not as individuals but in powerful and organized groups, a constitutional convention would, I fear, prove a witches' cauldron of class legislation and demagoguery. Is it not possible that modern democracy is in danger of strangulation by its present-day methods and ideals? Again the words of Washington suggest themselves: "If, to please the people, we offer what we ourselves disapprove, how can we afterwards defend our work? Let us raise a standard to which the wise and just can repair."

Working with a sad sincerity and with despair in their hearts, this little band of men wrought a work of surpassing importance, and if they did not receive the immediate plaudits of the living generation, their shades can at least solace themselves with the reflection that posterity has acclaimed their work as one of the greatest political achievements of man.

The rules of order and the nature of the proceedings thus determined, the convention opened by an address by Mr. Randolph of Virginia, in which he submitted, in the form of fifteen points—nearly the number of the fatal fourteen—the outlines for a new government. He himself in his opening speech summarized the propositions by candidly confessing "that they were not intended for a federal government" (thereby meaning a mere league of

States) but "a strong consolidated union." Upon this radical change the convention was to argue earnestly and at times bitterly for many a weary day. The plan provided for a national legislature of which the lower branch should be elected by the people and the upper branch by the lower branch upon the nomination of the legislatures of the States. This legislature should enjoy all the legislative rights given to the federation, and there followed the sweeping grant that it "could legislate in all cases to which the separate States are incompetent or in which the harmony of the United States may be interrupted by the exercise of individual legislation," with power "to negative all laws passed by the several States contravening in the opinion of the national legislature the Articles of the Union."

A national executive was proposed, together with a national judiciary, and these two bodies were given authority "to examine every act of the national legislature before it shall operate and every act of a particular legislature before a negative thereon shall be final." This marked an immense advance over the Articles of Confederation, under which there was no national executive or judiciary, and under which the legislature had no direct power over the citizens of the States, and could only impose duties upon the States themselves by the concurrence of nine of the thirteen.

Hardly had Mr. Randolph submitted the so-called Virginia plan when Charles Pinckney, of South Carolina, a young man of twenty-nine years of age, with the courage of youth submitted to the House a draft of the future federal government. Curiously enough, it did not differ in principle from the Virginia plan, but was more specific and concrete in stating the powers which the federal government should exercise, and many of its provisions were embodied in the final draft. Indeed, Pinckney's plan was the future Constitution of the United States in embryo; and when it is read and contrasted with the document which has so justly won the acclaim of men throughout the world, it is amazing that so young a man should have anticipated and reduced to a concrete and effective form many of the most novel features of the Federal Government. As the only copy of Pinckney's plan was furnished years afterwards to Madison for his journal, it is possible that some of its wisdom was of the post factum variety.

Having received the two plans, the convention then went, on May 30, into a committee of the whole to consider the fifteen propositions in the Virginia plan seriatim. They wisely concluded to determine abstract ideas first and concrete forms later. Apparently for the time being little attention was paid to Pinckney's plan, and this may have been due to the hostile attitude of the older members of the convention to the presumption of his youth.

Then ensued a very remarkable debate on the immediate propositions and the principles of government which underlay them, which lasted for two weeks. On June 13 the committee rose. Even the fragments of this debate, which may well have been one of the most notable in history, indicate the care with which the members had studied governments of ancient and modern times. There were many points of difference, but chief of them, which nearly resulted in the collapse of the convention, was the inevitable difficulty which always arises in the formation of a league of States or an association of nations between the great and the little States.

The five larger States had a population that was nearly twice as great as the remaining eight States. Thus Virginia's population was nearly ten-fold as great as Georgia. Moreover, the States differed greatly in their material wealth and power. Nevertheless, all of them entered the convention as independent sovereign nations, and the smaller nations contended that the equality in suffrage and political power which prevailed in the convention (in which each State, large or small, voted as a unit), should and must be preserved in the future government. To this the larger States were quite unwilling to yield, and when the committee rose they reported, in substance, the Virginia plan, with the proviso that representation in the proposed double-chambered Congress should be "according to some equitable ratio of representation."

On June 15 the small States presented their draft, which was afterwards known as the New Jersey plan, because it was introduced by Mr. Patterson of that State. It only contemplated an amendment to the existing Constitution and an amplification of the powers of the impotent Confederation. Its chief advance over the existing government was that it provided for a federal executive and a federal judiciary, but otherwise the government remained a mere league of States, in which the central government could generally act only by the vote of nine States, and in which their power was exhausted when they requested the States to enforce the decrees. Its chief advance over the Articles of Confederation, in addition to the creation of an executive, was an assertion that the acts of Congress "shall be the supreme law of the respective States ... and that the judiciary of the several States shall be bound thereby in their decisions," and that "if any State or any body of men in any State shall oppose or prevent the carrying into execution of such acts or treaties the federal executive shall be authorized to call forth the power of the confederated States ... to enforce and compel obedience to such acts or an observance of such treaties."

While this was some advance toward a truly national government, it yet left the national executive dependent upon the constituent States, for if they failed to respond to the call above stated the national government had no direct power over their citizens.

The New Jersey plan precipitated a crisis, and thereafter, and for many days, the argument proceeded, only to increase in bitterness.

On June 18 Alexander Hamilton, who agreed with no one else, addressed the convention for the first time. He spoke for five hours and reviewed exhaustively the Virginia and New Jersey plans, and possibly the Pinckney draft. Even the fragment of the speech, as taken in long-hand by Madison, shows that it was a masterly argument. He stated his belief "that the British Government was the best in the world and that he doubted much whether anything short of it would do in America." He praised the British Constitution, quoting Monsieur Necker as saying that "it was the only government in the world which unites government strength with individual security." He analysed and explained your Constitution as it then was and advocated an elective monarchy in form though not in name. It is true that he called the executive a "governor" and not a king, but the governor, so-called, was to serve for life and was given not only "a negative on all laws about to be passed," but even the execution of all duly enacted laws was in his discretion. The governor, with the consent of the Senate, was to make war, conclude all treaties, make all appointments, pardon all offences, with the full power through his negative of saying what laws should be passed and which enforced. Hamilton's governor would have been not dissimilar to Louis XIV, and could have said with him, "L'état, c'est moi!" The Senate also served for life, and the only concession which Hamilton made to democracy was an elective house of representatives. Thinly veiled, his plan contemplated an elective king with greater powers than those of George III, an imitation House of Lords and a popular House of Commons with a limited tenure.

Hamilton's plan was never taken seriously and, so far as the records show, was never afterwards considered. His admirers have given great praise to his work in the federal convention. His real contribution lay in the fact that when the Constitution was finally drafted and offered to the people, while he regarded it as a "wretched makeshift," to use his own expression, yet he was broad and patriotic enough to surrender his own views and advocate the adoption of the Constitution. In so doing, he fought a valorous fight, secured the acquiescence of the State of New York, and without its ratification the Constitution would never have been adopted. Hamilton later thought better of the Constitution, and its successful beginning is due in large measure to his genius for constructive administration.

As the debate proceeded, the crisis precipitated by the seemingly insoluble differences between the great and little States became more acute. The smaller States contended that the convention was transgressing its powers, and they demanded that the credentials of the various members be read. In this there was technical accuracy, for the delegates had been appointed to revise the Articles of Confederation and not to adopt a new Constitution. A majority of the convention, however, insisted upon the convention proceeding with the consideration of a new Constitution, and their views prevailed. It speaks well for the honour of the delegates that although their differences became so acute as to lead at times to bitter expressions, neither side divulged them to the outside public. The smaller States could easily have ended the convention by an appeal to public opinion, which was not then prepared for a "consolidated union," but they were loyal enough to fight out their quarrels within the walls of the convention hall.

At times the debate became bitter in the extreme. James Wilson, a delegate of Pennsylvania and a Scotchman by birth and education, turning to the representatives of the little States, passionately said:

"Will you abandon a country to which you are bound by so many strong and enduring ties? Should the event happen, it will neither stagger my sentiments nor duty. If the minority of the people refuse to coalesce with the majority on just and proper principles, if a separation must take place, it could never happen on better grounds."

He referred to the demand of the larger States that representation should be proportioned to the population. To this Bedford, of Delaware, as heatedly replied;

"We have been told with a dictatorial air that this is the last moment for a fair trial in favour of good government. It will be the last, indeed, if the propositions reported by the committee go forth to the people. The large States dare not dissolve the convention. If they do, the small ones will find some foreign ally of more honour and good faith, who will take them by the hand and do them justice."

Finally, the smaller States gave their ultimatum to the larger States that unless representation in both branches of the proposed legislature should be on the basis of equality—each State, whether large or small, having one vote—they would forthwith leave the convention. An eye-witness says that, at that moment, Washington, who was in the chair, gave old Doctor Franklin a significant look. Franklin arose and moved an adjournment for forty-eight hours, with the understanding that the delegates should confer with those with whom they disagreed rather than with those with whom they agreed.

A recess was taken, and when the convention re-convened on July 2, a vote was taken as to equality of representation in the Senate and resulted in a tie vote. It was then decided to appoint a committee of eleven, one from each State, to consider the question, and this committee reported three days later, on July 5, in favour of proportionate representation in the House and equal representation in the Senate. This suggestion, which finally saved the situation, was due to that wise old utilitarian philosopher, Franklin. Again, a vehement and passionate debate followed. Vague references were made to the sword as the only method of solving the difference.

On July 9 the committee again reported, maintaining the principle of their recommendation, while modifying its details, and the debate then turned upon the question to what extent the negro slaves should count in estimating population for the purposes of proportionate representation in the lower House. Various suggestions were made to base representation upon wealth or taxation and not upon population. For several days the debate lasted during very heated weather, but on the night of July 12 the temperature dropped and with it the emotional temperature of the delegates.

Some days previous, namely, June 28, when the debates were becoming so bitter that it seemed unlikely that the convention could continue, Doctor Franklin, erroneously supposed by many to be an atheist, made the following solemn and beautiful appeal to their better natures. He said:

"The small progress we have made after four or five weeks' close attendance and continual reasonings with each other—our different sentiments on almost every question, several of the last producing as many noes as ayes, is, methinks, a melancholy proof of the imperfection of the human understanding. We indeed seem to feel our own want of political wisdom, since we have been running about in search of it. We have gone back to ancient history for models of government, and examined the different forms of those Republics which, having been formed with the seeds of their own dissolution, now no longer exist. And we have viewed modern States all around Europe, but find none of their constitutions suitable to our circumstances.

"In this situation of this Assembly, groping as it were in the dark to find political truth, and scarce able to distinguish it when presented to us, how has it happened, sir, that we have not hitherto once thought of humbly applying to the Father of Lights to illuminate our understandings?... And have we now forgotten that powerful Friend or do we imagine that we no longer need His assistance? I have lived, sir, a long time, and the longer I live, the more convincing proofs I see of this truth: That God governs in the affairs of men. And if a sparrow cannot fall to the ground without His notice, is it probable that an empire can rise without His aid? We have been assured, sir, in the sacred writings, that 'except the Lord build the House they labour in vain that build it.' I firmly believe this; and I also believe that without His concurring aid we shall succeed in this political building no better than the builders of Babel. We shall be divided by our little partial local interests; our projects will be confounded, and we ourselves shall become a reproach and byword down to future ages. And what is worse, mankind may hereafter from this unfortunate instance, despair of establishing governments by human wisdom and leave it to chance, war, and conquest.

"I therefore beg leave to move that henceforth prayers imploring the assistance of Heaven, and its blessings on our deliberations, be held in this Assembly every morning before we proceed to business, and that one or more of the clergy of this city be requested to officiate in that service."

It may surprise my audience to know the sequel. The resolution was voted down, partly on the ground that if it became known to the public that the convention had finally resorted to prayers it might cause undue alarm, but also because the convention was by that time so low in funds that, as one of the members said, it did not have enough money to pay a clergyman his fees for the service. I suspect that their controlling reason was their indisposition to break their self-imposed rule of secrecy by contact with the outer world until their work was completed. Perhaps they thought that "God helps those who help themselves."

On July 16 the compromise was finally adopted of recognizing the claims of the larger States to proportionate representation in the House of Representatives, and recognizing the claims of the smaller States by according to them equal representation in the Senate. This great result was not effected without the first break in the convention, for the delegates from New York left in disgust and never returned, with the exception of Hamilton, who occasionally attended subsequent sessions. Such was the great concession that was made to secure the Constitution; and the only respect in which the Constitution to-day cannot be amended is that by express provision the equality of representation in the Senate shall never be disturbed. Thus it is that to-day some States, which have less population than some of the wards in the city of New York, have as many votes in the Senate as the great State of New York. It is unquestionably a palpable negation of majority rule, for as no measure can become a law without the concurrence of the Senate—now numbering ninety-six Senators—a combination of the little States, whoso aggregate population is not a fifth of the American people, can defeat the will of the remaining four-fifths. Pennsylvania and New York, with nearly one-sixth of the entire population of the United States, have only four votes in ninety-six votes in the Senate.

Fortunately, political alignments have rarely been between the greater and the smaller States exclusively. Their equality in the Senate was a big price to pay for the Union, but, as the event has shown, not too great.

The convention next turned its attention to the Executive and the manner of its selection, and upon this point there was the widest contrariety of view, but, fortunately, without the acute feeling that the relative power of the States had occasioned.

Then the judiciary article was taken up, and there was much earnest discussion as to whether the new Constitution should embody the French idea of giving to the judiciary, in conjunction with the Executive, a revisory power over legislation. Three times the convention voted upon this dangerous proposition, and on one occasion it was only defeated by a single vote. Fortunately, the good sense of the convention rejected a proposition, that had caused in France constant conflicts between the Executive and the Judiciary, by substituting the right of the President to veto congressional legislation, with the right of Congress, by a two-thirds vote of each House, to override the veto, and secondly by an implied power in the Judiciary to annul Congressional or State legislation, not on the grounds of policy, but on the sole ground of inconsistency with the paramount law of the Constitution. In this adjustment, the influence of Montesquieu was evident. These and many practical details had resulted in an expansion of the fifteen proposals of the Virginia plan to twenty-three.

Having thus determined the general principles that should guide them in their labours, the convention, on July 26 appointed a Committee on Detail to embody these propositions in the formal draft of a Constitution and adjourned until August 6 to await its report. That report, when finally completed, covered seven folio pages, and was found to consist of a Preamble and twenty-three Articles, embodying forty-three sections. The draft did not slavishly follow the Virginia propositions, for the committee embodied some valuable suggestions which had occurred to them in their deliberations. Nevertheless, it substantially put the Virginia plan into a workable plan which proved to be the Constitution of the United States in embryo.

When the committee on detail had made its report on August 6, the convention proceeded for over a month to debate it with the most minute care. Every day for five weeks, for five hours each day, the members studied and debated with meticulous care every sentence of the proposed Constitution. Time does not suffice even for the barest statement of the many interesting questions which were thus discussed, but they nearly ran the whole gamut of constitutional government. Many fanciful ideas were suggested but with unvarying good sense they were rejected. Some of the results were, under the circumstances, curious. For example, although it was a convention of comparatively young men, and although the convention could have taken into account the many successful young men in public life in Europe—as, for example, William Pitt—they put a disqualification upon age by providing that a Representative must be twenty-five years of age, a Senator thirty years of age, and a President thirty-five years of age. When it was suggested that young men could learn by admission to public life, the sententious reply was made that, while they could, they ought not to have their education at the public expense.

The debates proceeded, however, in better temper, and almost the only question that again gave rise to passionate argument was that of slavery. The extreme Southern States declared that they would never accept the new plan "except the right to import slaves be untouched." This question was finally compromised by agreeing that the importation of slaves should end after the year 1808. It however left the slave population then existing in a state of bondage, and for this necessary compromise the nation seventy-five years later was to pay dearly by one of the most destructive civil wars in the annals of mankind.

August was now drawing to a close. The convention had been in session for more than three months. Of its work the public knew nothing, and this notwithstanding the acute interest which the American people, not merely facing the peril of anarchy, but actually suffering from it, must have taken in the convention. Its vital importance was not under-estimated. While its builders, like all master builders, did "build better than they knew," yet it cannot be said that they under-estimated the importance of their labours. As one of their number, Gouveneur Morris said: "The whole human race will be affected by the proceedings of this convention." After it adjourned one of its greatest participants, James Wilson, of Pennsylvania, said:

"After the lapse of six thousand years since the creation of the world, America now presents the first instance of a people assembled to say deliberately and calmly and to decide leisurely and peaceably on the form of government by which they will bind themselves and their posterity."

In the absence of any authentic information, the rumour spread through the colonies that the convention was about to reconstitute a monarchy by inviting the second son of George III, the Bishop of Osnaburg, to be King of the United States; and these rumours became so persistent as to evoke from the silent convention a semi-official denial. There is some reason to believe that a minority of the convention did see in the restoration of a constitutional monarchy the only solution of the problem.

On September 8 the committee had finally considered and, after modifications, approved the draft of the Committee on Detail, and a new committee was thereupon appointed "to revise the style of and arrange the articles that had been agreed to by the House." This committee was one of exceptional strength. There were Dr. William Samuel Johnson, a graduate of Oxford and a friend of his great namesake, Samuel Johnson; Alexander Hamilton, Gouveneur Morris, a brilliant mind with an unusual gift for lucid expression; James Madison, a true scholar in politics, and Rufus King, an orator who, in the inflated language of the day, "was ranked among the luminaries of the present age."

The convention then adjourned to await the final revision of the draft by the Committee on Style.

On September 12 the committee reported. While it is not certain, it is believed that its work was largely that of Gouveneur Morris.

September 13 the printed copies of the report of the Committee on Style were ready, and three more days were spent by the convention in carefully comparing each article and section of this final draft.

On September 15 the work of drafting the Constitution was regarded as ended, and it was adopted and ordered to be engrossed for signing.

It may be interesting at this point to give the result of their labours as measured in words, and if the framers of the Constitution deserve the plaudits of posterity in no other respect they do in the remarkable self-restraint which those results revealed.

The convention had been in session for 81 continuous days. Probably they had consumed over 300 hours in debate. If their debates had been fully reported, they would probably have filled at least fifty volumes, and yet the net result of their labours consisted of about 4,000 words, 89 sentences, and about 140 distinct provisions. As the late Lord Bryce, speaking in this age of unbridled expression, both oral and printed, so well has said:

"The Constitution of the United States, including the amendments, may be read aloud in twenty-three minutes. It is about half as long as Saint Paul's Epistle to the Corinthians, and one-fourth as long as the Irish Land Act of 1881. History knows few instruments which in so few words lay down equally momentous rules on a vast range of matters of the highest importance and complexity."

Even including the nineteen amendments, the Constitution, after one hundred and thirty-five years of development, does not exceed 7,000 words. What admirable self-restraint! Possibly single opinions of the Supreme Court could be cited which are as long as the whole document of which they are interpreting a single phrase. This does not argue that the Constitution is an obscure document, for it would be difficult to cite any political document in the annals of mankind that was so simple and lucid in expression. There is nothing Johnsonese about its style. Every word is a word of plain speech, the ordinary meaning of which even the man in the street knows. No tautology is to be found and no attempt at ornate expression. It is a model of simplicity, and as it flows through the reaches of history it will always excite the admiration of those who love clarity and not rhetorical excesses. One can say of it as Horace said of his favourite Spring: O, fons Bandusiae, splendidior vitro. Dulce digne mero, non sine floribus.

If I be asked why, if this be true, it has required many lengthy opinions of the Supreme Court in the 256 volumes of its Reports to interpret its meaning, the answer is that, as with the simple sayings of the great Galilean, whose words have likewise been the subject of unending commentary, the question is not one of clarity but of adaptation of the meaning to the ever-changing conditions of human life. Moreover, as with the sayings of the Master or the unequalled verse of Shakespeare, questions of construction are more due to the commentators than to the text itself.

On September 17 the convention met for the last time. The document was engrossed and laid before the members for signature. Of the fifty-five members who had attended, only thirty-nine remained. Of those, a number were unwilling to sign as individuals. While the members had not been unconscious of the magnitude of their labours, they were quite insensible of the magnitude of their achievement. Few there were of the convention who were enthusiastic about this result. Indeed, as the document was ready for signature, it became a grave question whether the remnant which remained had sufficient faith in their own work to subscribe their names, and if they failed to do so its adoption by the people would have been impossible. It was then that Doctor Franklin rendered one of the last and greatest services of his life. With ingratiating wit and with all the impressiveness that his distinguished career inspired, Franklin thus spoke:

"I confess that there are several parts of this Constitution which I do not at present approve, but I am not sure I shall never approve them. For having lived long I have experienced many instances of being obliged by better information or fuller consideration, to change opinions even on important subjects, which I once thought right, but found to be otherwise. It is therefore that the older I grow, the more apt I am to doubt my own judgment and to pay more respect to the judgment of others. Most men indeed as well as most sects in religion think themselves in possession of all truth, and that wherever others differ from them it is so far error. Steele, a Protestant, in a dedication tells the Pope that the only difference between our Churches in their opinions of the certainty of their doctrines is, the Church of Rome is infallible and the Church of England is never in the wrong. But though many private persons think almost as highly of their own infallibility as of that of their sect, few express it so naturally as a certain French lady, who in a dispute with her sister, said: 'I don't know how it happens, sister, but I meet with nobody but myself that's always in the right.'—Il n'y a que moi qui a toujours raison.

"In these sentiments, sir, I agree to this Constitution with all its faults, if they are such; because I think a general government necessary for us, and there is no form of government but what may be a blessing to the people, if well administered, and I believe further that this is likely to be well administered for a course of years, and can only end in despotism as other forms have done before it, when the people shall become so corrupted as to need despotic government, being incapable of any other. I doubt, too, whether any other convention we can obtain may be able to make a better Constitution. For when you assemble a number of men to have the advantage of their joint wisdom you inevitably assemble with those men all their prejudices, their passions, their errors of opinion, their local interests, and their selfish views. From such an assembly can a perfect production be expected? It therefore astonishes me, sir, to find this system approaching so near to perfection as it does.... Thus, I consent, sir, to this Constitution because I expect no better, and because I am not sure that it is not the best. The opinions I have had of its errors I sacrifice to the public good, I have never whispered a syllable of them abroad. Within these walls they were born and here they shall die. If every one of us in returning to our constituents were to report the objections he has had to it and endeavour to gain partisans in support of them, we might prevent its being generally received, and thereby lost all the salutary effects and great advantages resulting naturally in our favour among foreign nations as well as among ourselves from our real or apparent unanimity.

"On the whole, sir, I cannot help expressing a wish that every member of the convention who may still have objections to it, would with me, on this occasion doubt a little of his own infallibility—and to make manifest our unanimity, put his name to this instrument."

Truly this spirit of Doctor Franklin could be profitably invoked in this day and generation, when nations are so intolerant of the ideas of other nations.

As the members, moved by Franklin's humorous and yet moving appeal, came forward to subscribe their names, Franklin drew the attention of some of the members to the fact that on the back of the President's chair was the half disk of a sun, and, with his love of metaphor, he said that painters had often found it difficult to distinguish in their art a rising from a setting sun. He then prophetically added:

"I have often and often in the course of the sessions and the vicissitudes of my hopes and fears in its issues, looked at that behind the President without being able to tell whether it was rising or setting. But now at length I have the happiness to know that it is a rising and not a setting sun."

Time has verified the genial doctor's prediction. The career of the new nation thus formed has hitherto been a rising and not a setting sun. He had in his sixty years of conspicuously useful citizenship—and perhaps no nation ever had a more untiring and unselfish servant—done more than any American to develop the American Commonwealth, but like Moses, he was destined to see the promised land only from afar, for the new Government had hardly been inaugurated, before Franklin died, as full of years as honours. Prophetic as was his vision, he could never have anticipated the reality of to-day, for this nation, thus deliberately formed in the light of reason and without blood or passion, is to-day, by common consent, one of the greatest and, I trust I may add, one of the noblest republics of all time.

THE POLITICAL PHILOSOPHY OF THE
CONSTITUTION

In my last address I left Doctor Franklin predicting to the discouraged remnant of the constitutional convention that the nation then formed would be a "rising sun" in the constellation of the nations. The sun, however, was destined to rise through a bank of dark and murky clouds, for the Constitution could not take effect until it was ratified by nine of the thirteen States; and when it was submitted to the people, who selected State conventions for the purpose of ratifying or rejecting the proposed plan of government, a bitter controversy at once ensued between two political parties, then in process of formation, one called the Constitution ratified without controversy. In the remaining ten the struggle was long and arduous, and nearly a year passed before the requisite nine States gave their assent. Two of the States refused to become parts of the new nation, even after it began, and three years passed before the thirteen States were re-united under the Constitution.

It could not have been ratified had there not been an assurance that there would be immediate amendments to provide a Bill of Rights to safeguard the individual. Thus came into existence the first ten amendments to the Constitution, with their perpetual guaranty of the fundamental rights of religion, freedom of speech and of the Press, the right of assemblage, the immunity from unreasonable searches and seizures, the right of trial by jury, and similar guarantees of fundamental individual rights.

Distrustful as the American people were of the new Constitution, they yet had the political sagacity to prefer its imperfections, whatever they imagined them to be, to the mad spirit of innovation; and in order that the great instrument should not, through the excesses of party passion or the temporary caprices of fleeting generations, speedily become a mere "scrap of paper" they very wisely provided that no amendment should, in the future, be made unless it was proposed by at least two-thirds of the Senate and the House of Representatives and ratified by three-fourths of the States through their legislatures or through special conventions. This was only one of many striking negations of the principle of majority rule. As a result of this provision, if we count the first ten amendments as virtually part of the original document, only nine amendments have been adopted in 185 years, and of these, excepting the amendments which ended slavery as the result of the Civil War, only the last three, passed in recent years partly through the relaxing influence of the world war, mark a serious departure from the basic principles of the Constitution.

This stability is the more remarkable when we recall the profound and revolutionary change that has taken place in the social life of man since the Constitution was adopted. It was framed at the very end of the pastoral-agricultural age of humanity. The industrial revolution, which has more profoundly affected man in the last century and a half than all the changes which had theretofore taken place in the life of man since the cave-dweller, was only then beginning. Measured in terms of mechanical power, men when the Constitution was formed were Lilliputians as compared with the Brobdingnagians of our day, when man outflies the eagle, outswims the fish, and by his conquest and utilization of the invisible forces of nature has become the superman; and yet the Constitution of 1787 is, in most of its essential principles, still the Constitution of 1922. This surely marks it as a marvel in statecraft and can only be explained by the fact that the Constitution was developed by a people who, as "children brave and free of the great mother-tongue," had a real genius for self-government and its essential element, the spirit of self-restraint.

While it is true that the text of the instrument has suffered almost as little change as the Nicene Creed, yet it would be manifest error to suggest that in its development by practical application the Constitution has not undergone great changes.

The first and greatest of all its expounders, Chief Justice Marshall, said, in one of his greatest opinions, that the Constitution was—

"intended to endure for ages to come, and consequently to be adapted to the various crises of human affairs. To have prescribed the means by which government should in all future times execute its powers would have been to change entirely the character of the instrument and to give it the properties of a legal code. It would have been an unwise attempt to provide by immutable rules for exigencies which, if foreseen at all, must have been foreseen dimly, and can best be provided for as they occur."

In this great purpose of enumerating rather than defining the powers of government its framers were supremely wise. While it was marvellously sagacious in what it provided, it was wise to the point of inspiration in what it left unprovided.

Nothing is more admirable than the self-restraint of men who, venturing upon an untried experiment, and after debating for four months upon the principles of government, were content to embody their conclusions in not more than four thousand words. To this we owe the elasticity of the instrument. Its vitality is due to the fact that, by usage, judicial interpretation, and, when necessary, formal amendment, it can be thus adapted to the ever-accelerating changes of the most progressive age in history, and that a people have administered the Constitution who, in the process of such adaptation, have generally shown the same spirit of conservative self-restraint as did the men who framed it.

The Constitution is neither, on the one hand, a Gibraltar rock, which wholly resists the ceaseless washing of time or circumstance, nor is it, on the other hand, a sandy beach, which is slowly destroyed by the erosion of the waves. It is rather to be likened to a floating dock, which, while firmly attached to its moorings, and not therefore the caprice of the waves, yet rises and falls with the tide of time and circumstance.

While in its practical adaptation to this complex age the men who framed it, if they could "revisit the glimpses of the moon," would as little recognize their own handiwork as their own nation, yet they would still be able to find in successful operation the essential principles which they embodied in the document more than a century ago.

Its success is also due to the fact that its framers were little influenced by the spirit of doctrinarianism. They were not empiricists, but very practical men. This is the more remarkable because they worked in a period of an emotional fermentation of human thought. The long-repressed intellect of man had broken into a violent eruption like that of a seemingly extinct volcano.

From the middle of the eighteenth century until the end of the French Revolution the masses everywhere were influenced by the emotional, and at times hysterical, abstractions of the French encyclopedists; and that these had influenced thought in the American colonies is readily shown in the preamble of the Declaration of Independence, with its unqualified assertion of the equality of men and the absolute right of self-determination. The Declaration sought in its noble idealism to make the "world safe for democracy," but the Constitution attempted the greater task of making democracy safe for the world by inducing a people to impose upon themselves salutary restraints upon majority rule.

Fortunately, the framers of the Constitution had learned a rude and terrible lesson in the anarchy that had followed the War of Independence. They were not so much concerned about the rights of man as about his duties, and their great purpose was to substitute for the visionary idealism of a rampant individualism the authority of law. Of the hysteria of that time, which was about to culminate in the French Revolution, there is no trace in the Constitution.

They were less concerned about Rousseau's social contract than to restore law and order. Hard realities and not generous and impossible abstractions interested them. They had suffered grievously for more than ten years from misrule and had a distaste for mere phrase-making, of which they had had a satiety, for the Constitution, in which there is not a wasted word, is as cold and dry a document as a problem in mathematics or a manual of parliamentary law. Its mandates have the simplicity and directness of the Ten Commandments, and, like the Decalogue, it consists more of what shall not be done than what shall be done. In this freedom from empiricism and sturdy adherence to the realities of life, it can be profitably commended to all nations which may attempt a similar task.

While the Constitution apparently only deals with the practical and essential details of government, yet underlying these simply but wonderfully phrased delegations of power is a broad and accurate political philosophy, which goes far to state the "law and the prophets" of free government.

These essential principles of the Constitution may be briefly summarized as follows:

CHAPTER I.

The first is representative government.

Nothing is more striking in the debates of the convention than the distrust of its members, with few exceptions, of what they called "democracy." By this term they meant the power of the people to legislate directly and without the intervention of chosen representatives. They believed that the utmost concession that could be safely made to democracy was the power to select suitable men to legislate for the common good, and nothing is more striking in the Constitution than the care with which they sought to remove the powers of legislation from the direct action of the people. Nowhere in the instrument is there a suggestion of the initiative or referendum.

Even an amendment to the Constitution could not be directly proposed by the people in the exercise of their residual power or adopted by them. As previously said, it could only be proposed by two-thirds of the House and the Senate, and then could only become effective, if ratified by three-fourths of the States, acting, not by a popular vote, but through their chosen representatives either in their legislatures or special conventions. Thus they denied the power of a majority to alter even the form of government. Moreover, they gave to the President the power to nullify laws passed by a majority of the House and Senate by his simple veto, and yet, fearful of an unqualified power of the President in this respect, they provided that the veto itself should be vetoed, if two-thirds of the Senate and House concurred in such action. Moreover, the great limitations of the Constitution, which forbid the majority, or even the whole body of the House and Senate, to pass laws either for want of authority or because they impair fundamental rights of individuals, are as emphatic a negation of an absolute democracy as can be found in any form of government.

Measured by present-day conventions of democracy, the Constitution is an undemocratic document. The framers believed in representative government, to which they gave the name "Republicanism" as the antithesis to "democracy." The members of the Senate were to be selected by State legislatures, and the President himself was, as originally planned, to be selected by an electoral college similar to the College of Cardinals.

The debates are full of utterances which explain this attitude of mind. Mr. Gerry said: "The evils we experience flow from the excesses of democracy. The people are the dupes of pretended patriots." Mr. Randolph, the author of the Virginia plan, observed that the general object of the Constitution was to provide a cure for the evils under which the United States laboured; that in tracing these evils to their origin every man had found it in the tribulation and follies of democracy; that some check, therefore, was to be sought for against this tendency of our Government.

Alexander Hamilton remarked, on June 18, that—

"the members most tenacious of republicanism were as loud as any in declaiming against the evils of democracy."

He added:

"Give all the power to the many and they will oppress the few. Give all the power to the few and they will oppress the many. Both ought, therefore, to have the power that each may defend itself against the other."

Perhaps the attitude of the members is thus best expressed by James Madison, in the 10th of the Federalist papers:

"A pure democracy, by which I mean a State consisting of a small number of citizens, who assemble and administer the government in person, can admit of no cure for the mischiefs of faction. Such democracies have ever been spectacles of turbulence and contention, and have often been found incompatible with the personal security and rights of property, and have generally been as short in their lives as they have been violent in their deaths."

Undoubtedly, the framers of the Constitution in thus limiting popular rule did not take sufficient account of the genius of an English-speaking people. A few of their number recognized this. Franklin, a self-made man, believed in democracy and doubted the efficacy of the Constitution unless it was, like a pyramid, broad-based upon the will of the people.

Colonel Mason, of Virginia, who was also of the Jeffersonian school of political philosophy, said:

"Notwithstanding the oppression and injustice experienced among us from democracy, the genius of the people is in favour of it, and the genius of the people must be consulted."

In this they were true prophets, for the American people have refused to limit democracy as narrowly and rigidly as the framers of the Constitution clearly intended. The most notable illustration of this is the selection of the President. It was never contemplated that the people should directly select the President, but that a chosen body of electors should, with careful deliberation, make this momentous choice. While, in form, the system persists to this day, from the very beginning the electors simply vote as the people who select them desire. It should here be noted that Thomas Jefferson, the great Democrat and draftsman of the Declaration of Independence, was not a member of the convention. During its sessions he was in France. He was instrumental in securing the first ten Amendments and the subsequent adaptation of the Constitution to meet the democratic instincts of the American people is largely due to his great leadership.

Moreover, the spirit of representative government has greatly changed since the Constitution was adopted. The ideal of the earlier time was that so nobly expressed by Edmund Burke in his address to the electors of Bristol, for the framers believed that a representative held a judicial position of the most sacred character, and that he should vote as his judgment and conscience dictated without respect to the wishes of his constituents. To-day, and notably in the last half century, the contrary belief, due largely to Jefferson's political ideals, has so influenced American politics that the representatives of the people, either in the legislature or the executive departments of the government, are considered by the masses as only the mouthpieces of the people who select them, and to ignore their wishes is regarded as virtually a betrayal of a trust and the negation of democracy.

For this change in attitude there has been much justification, for in my country, as elsewhere, the people do not always select their best men as representatives, and, with the imperfections of human nature, there has been so much of ignorance and, at times, venality, that the instinct of the people is to take the conduct of affairs into their own hands. On the other hand, this change of attitude has led, in many instances, to government by organized minorities, for, with the division of the masses into political parties, it is easy for an organized minority to hold the balance of power, and thus impress its will upon majorities. Time may yet vindicate the theory of the framers that the limit of democracy is the selection of true and tried representatives.

CHAPTER II.

The second and most novel principle of the Constitution is its dual form of Government.

This did constitute a unique contribution to the science of politics. This was early recognized by de Tocqueville, one of the most acute students of the Constitution, who said that it was based "upon a wholly, novel theory, which may be considered a great discovery in modern political science."

Previous to the Constitution it had not been thought possible to divide sovereignty, or at least to have two different sovereignties moving as planets in the same orbit. Therefore, all previous federated governments had been based upon the plan that a league could only effect its will through the constituent States and that the citizens in these States owed no direct allegiance to the league, but only to the States of which they were members. The Constitution, however, developed the idea of a dual citizenship. While the people remained citizens of their respective States in the sphere of government which was reserved to the States, yet they directly became citizens of the central government, and, as such, ceased to be citizens of the several States in the sphere of government delegated to the central power; and this allegiance was enforced by the direct action of the central government on the citizens as individuals. Thus has been developed one of the most intricately complex governmental systems in the world.

At the time of the adoption of the Constitution this division of jurisdiction was quite feasible, for, geographically, the various States were widely separated, and the lack of economic contact made it easy for each government to function without serious conflict. The framers, however, did not sufficiently reckon with the mechanical changes in society that were then beginning. They did not anticipate, and could not have anticipated, the centripetal influences of steam and electricity which have woven the American people into an indissoluble unit for commercial and many other purposes. As a result many laws of the Federal Government, in their incidences in this complex age, directly impinge upon rights of the State governments, and vice versa, and the practical application of the Constitution has required a very subtle adaptation of a form of government which was enacted in a primitive age to a form of government of a complex age.

Take, for example, the power over commerce. According to the Constitution, the Federal Government had plenary power over foreign commerce and commerce between the States, but the power over commerce within a State was reserved to State governments. This presupposed the power of Government to divide commerce into two water-tight compartments, or, at least, to regard the two spheres of power as parallel lines that would never meet; whereas with the coming of the railroad, steamship and the telegraph commerce has become so unified that the parallel lines have become lines of interlacing zigzags. To adapt the commerce clause of the Constitution to these changed conditions has required, in the highest degree, the constructive genius of the Supreme Court of the United States, and, in a series of very remarkable decisions, which are contained in 256 volumes of the official reports, that great tribunal has tried to draw a line between inter-State and domestic commerce as nearly to the original plans of the framers as it was possible; but obviously there has been so much adaptation to make this possible that if Washington, Franklin, Madison and Hamilton could revisit the nation they created they would not recognize their own handiwork.

For the same reason, the dual system of government has been profoundly modified by the great elemental forces of our mechanical age, so that the scales, which try to hold in nice equipoise the Federal Government on the one hand and the States on the other, have been greatly disturbed. Originally, the States were the powerful political entities, and the central government a mere agent for certain specific purposes; but, in the development of the Constitution, the nation has naturally become of overshadowing importance, while the States have relatively steadily diminished in power and prestige.

These inevitable tendencies in American politics are called "centralization," and while for nearly a century a great political party bitterly contested its steady progress, due to the centripetal influences above indicated, yet the contest was long since abandoned as a hopeless one, and the struggle to-day is rather to keep, so far as possible, the inevitable tendency measurably in check.

Nevertheless, it would be erroneous to suggest that the dual system of government is a failure. It still endures in providing a large measure of authority to the States in their purely domestic concerns, and, in a country that extends from the Atlantic to the Pacific, and from the Lakes to the Gulf, whose northern border is not very far from the Arctic Circle, and whose southern border is not many degrees from the Equator, there are such differences in the habits, conventions, and ideals of the people that without this dual form of government the Constitution would long since have broken down. It is not too much to say that the success with which the framers of the Constitution reconciled national supremacy and efficiency with local self-government is one of the great achievements in the history of mankind.

CHAPTER III.

The third principle was the guaranty of individual liberty through constitutional limitations.

This marked another great contribution of America to the science of government. In all previous government building, the State was regarded as a sovereign, which could grant to individuals or classes, out of its plenary power, certain privileges or exemptions, which were called "liberties." Thus the liberties which the barons wrung from King John at Runnymede were virtually exemptions from the power of government. Our fathers did not believe in the sovereignty of the State in the sense of absolute power, nor did they believe in the sovereignty of the people in that sense. The word "sovereignty" will not be found in the Constitution or the Declaration of Independence. They believed that each individual, as a responsible moral being, had certain "inalienable rights" which neither the State nor the people could rightfully take from him.

This conception of individualism, enforced in courts of law against executives and legislatures, was wholly new and is the distinguishing characteristic of American constitutionalism. As to such reserved rights, guaranteed by Constitutional limitations, and largely by the first ten amendments to the Constitution, a man, by virtue of his inherent and God-given dignity as a human soul, has rights, such as freedom of the Press, liberty of speech, property rights, and religious freedom, which even one hundred millions of people cannot rightfully take from him, without amending the Constitution. The framers did not believe that the oil of anointing that was supposed to sanctify the monarch and give him infallibility had fallen upon the "multitudinous tongue" of the people to give it either infallibility or omnipotence. They believed in individualism. They were animated by a sleepless jealousy of governmental power. They believed that the greater such power, the greater the danger of its abuse. They felt that the individual could generally best work out his own salvation, and that his constant prayer to Government was that of Diogenes to Alexander: "Keep out of my sunlight." The worth and dignity of the human soul, the free competition of man and man, the nobility of labour, the right to work, free from the tyranny of state or class, this was their gospel. Socialism was to them abhorrent.

This theory of government gave a new dignity to manhood. It said to the State: "There is a limit to your power. Thus far and no further, and here shall thy proud waves be stayed."

CHAPTER IV.

Closely allied to this doctrine of limited governmental powers, even by a majority, is the fourth principle of an independent judiciary.

It is the balance wheel of the Constitution, and to function it must be beyond the possibility of attack and destruction. My country was founded upon the rock of property rights and the sanctity of contracts. Both the nation and the several States are forbidden to impair the obligation of contracts, or take away life, liberty, or property "without due process of law." The guarantee is as old as Magna Charta; for "due process of law" is but a paraphrase of "the law of the land," without which no freeman could be deprived of his liberties or possessions.

"Due process of law" means that there are certain fundamental principles of liberty, not defined or even enumerated in the Constitution, but having their sanction in the free and enlightened conscience of just men, and that no man can be deprived of life, liberty, or property, except in conformity with these fundamental decencies of liberty. To protect these even against the will of a majority, however large, the judiciary was given unprecedented powers. It threw about the individual the solemn circle of the law. It made the judiciary the final conscience of the nation. Your nation cherishes the same primal verities of liberty, but with you, the people in Parliament, is the final judge. We, however, are not content that a majority of the Legislature shall override inviolable individual rights, about which the judiciary is empowered to throw the solemn circle of the law.

This august power has won the admiration of the world, and by many is regarded as a novel contribution to the science of government. The idea, however, was not wholly novel. As previously shown, four Chief Justices of England had declared that an Act of Parliament, if against common right and reason, could be treated as null and void; while in France the power of the judiciary to refuse efficacy to a law, unless sanctioned by the judiciary, had been the cause of a long struggle for at least three centuries between the French monarch and the courts of France. However, in England the doctrine of the common law yielded to the later doctrine of the omnipotence of Parliament, while in France the revisory power of the judiciary was terminated by the French Revolution.

The United States, however, embodied it in its form of government and thus made the judiciary, and especially the Supreme Court, the balance wheel of the Constitution. Without such power the Constitution could never have lasted, for neither executive officers nor legislatures are good judges of the extent of their own powers.

Nothing more strikingly shows the spirit of unity which the Constitution brought into being than the unbroken success with which the Supreme Court has discharged this difficult and most delicate duty. The President is the Commander-in-Chief of the Army and the Navy and can call them to his aid. The legislature has almost unlimited power through its control of the public purse. The States have their power reinforced by armed forces, and some of them are as great in population and resources as many of the nations of Europe. The Supreme Court, however, has only one officer to execute its decrees, called the United States Marshal; and yet, without sword or purse, and with only a high sheriff to enforce its mandates, when the Supreme Court says to a President or to a Congress or to the authorities of a great—and, in some respects, sovereign—State that they must do this or must refrain from doing that, the mandate is at once obeyed. Here, indeed, is the American ideal of "a government of laws and not of men" most strikingly realized; and if the American Constitution, as formulated and developed, had done nothing else than to establish in this manner the supremacy of law, even as against the overwhelming sentiment of the people, it would have justified the well-known encomium of Mr. Gladstone. It must be added, however, that in one respect this function of the judiciary has had an unfortunate effect in lessening rather than developing in the people the sense of constitutional morality. In your country the power of Parliament is omnipotent, and yet in its legislation it voluntarily observes these great fundamental decencies of liberty which in the American Constitution are protected by formal guarantees. This can only be true because either your representatives in Parliament have a deep sense of constitutional morality, or that the constituencies which select them have so much sense of constitutional justice that their representatives dare not disregard these fundamental decencies of liberty.

In the United States, however, the confidence that the Supreme Court will itself protect these guaranties of liberty has led to a diminution of the sense of constitutional morality, both in the people and their representatives. It abates the vigilance which is said to be ever the price of liberty.

Laws are passed which transgress the limitations of the Constitution without adequate discussion as to their unconstitutional character, for the reason that the determination of this fact is erroneously supposed to be the exclusive function of the judiciary.

The judiciary, contrary to the common supposition, has no plenary power to nullify unconstitutional laws. It can only do so when there is an irreconcilable and indubitable repugnancy between a law and the Constitution; but obviously laws can be passed from motives that are anti-constitutional, and there is a wide sphere of political discretion in which many acts can be done which, while politically anti-constitutional, are not juridically unconstitutional. For this reason, the undue dependence upon the judiciary to nullify every law which either in form, necessary operation, or motive transgresses the Constitution has so far lessened the vigilance of the people to protect their own Constitution as to lead to its serious impairment.

CHAPTER V.

The fifth fundamental principle was a system of governmental checks and balances.

The founders of the Republic were not enamoured of power. As they viewed human history, the worst evils of government were due to excessive concentration of power, which like Othello's jealousy "makes the meat it feeds on."

This system of checks and balances again illustrates that the Constitution is the great negation of unrestrained democracy. The framers believed that a people was best governed that was least governed. Therefore, their purpose was not so much to promote efficiency in legislation as to put a brake upon precipitate action.

Time does not suffice to state the intricate system of checks and balances whereby the legislature acts as a check upon the executive and the executive upon the legislature, and the Supreme Court upon both. When the Republic was small, and its public affairs were few, this system of checks and balances worked admirably, but to-day, when the nation is one of the greatest in the world, and its public affairs are of the most important and complicated character, and often require speedy action, it may be questioned whether the system is not now an undue brake upon governmental efficiency, and does not require some modification to ensure efficiency. Indeed, it is a serious question with many thoughtful Americans whether the growth of the United States has not put an excessive strain upon its governmental machinery.

This system was in part due to the confident belief of the framers of the Constitution in the Montesquieu doctrine of the division of government into three independent departments—legislative, executive and judicial; but experience has shown how difficult it is to apply this doctrine in its literal rigidity. One result of the doctrine was the mistaken attempt to keep the legislative and the executive as far apart as possible. The Cabinet system of parliamentary government was not adopted. While the President can appear before Congress and express his views, his Cabinet is without such right. In practice, the gulf is bridged by constant contact between the Cabinet and the committees of Congress, but this does not wholly secure speedy and efficient co-operation between the two departments. As I speak, a movement is in progress, with the sanction of President Harding, to permit members of his Cabinet to appear in Congress and thus defend directly and in person the policies of the Executive.

This separation of the two departments, which causes so much friction, has been emphasized by one feature of the Constitution which again marks its distrust of democracy, namely the fixed tenure of office. The Constitution did not intend that public officials should rise or fall with the fleeting caprices of a constituency. It preferred to give the President and the members of Congress a fixed term of office, and, however unpopular they might become temporarily, they should have the right and the opportunity to proceed even with unpopular policies, and thus challenge the final verdict of the people.

If a parliamentary form of government, immediately responsive to current opinion as registered in elections, is the great desideratum, then the fixed tenure of offices is the vulnerable Achilles-heel of our form of government. In other countries the Executive cannot survive a vote of want of confidence by the legislature. In America, the President, who is merely the Executive of the legislative will, continues for his prescribed term, though he may have wholly lost the confidence of the representatives of the people in Congress. While this makes for stability in administration and keeps the ship of state on an even keel, yet it also leads to the fatalism of our democracy, and often the "native hue" of its resolution is thus "sicklied o'er with the pale cast of thought." Take a striking instance. I am confident that after the sinking of the Lusitania, the United States would have entered the world war, if President Wilson's tenure of power had then depended upon a vote of confidence.

CHAPTER VI.

The sixth fundamental principle is the joint power of the Senate and the Executive over the foreign relations of the Government.

I need not dwell at length upon this unique feature of our constitutional system, for since the Versailles Treaty, the world has become well acquainted with our peculiar system under which treaties are made and war is declared or terminated. Nothing, excepting the principle of local rule, was of deeper concern to the framers of the Constitution. When it was framed, it was the accepted principle of all other nations that the control of the foreign relations of the Government was the exclusive prerogative of the Executive. In your country the only limitation upon that power was the control of Parliament over the purse of the nation, and some of the great struggles in your history related to the attempt of the Crown to exact money to carry on the wars without a Parliament grant.

The framers were unwilling to lodge any such power in the Executive, however great his powers in other respects. This was primarily due to the conception of the States that then prevailed. While they had created a central government for certain specified purposes, they yet regarded themselves as sovereign nations, and their representatives in the Senate were, in a sense, their ambassadors. They were as little inclined to permit the President of the United States to make treaties or declare war at will in their behalf as the European nations would be to-day to vest a similar authority in the League of Nations. It was, therefore, first proposed that the power to make treaties and appoint diplomatic representatives should be vested exclusively in the Senate, but as that body was not always in session, this plan was so far modified as to give the President, who is always acting, the power to negotiate treaties "with the advice and consent of the Senate." As to making war, the framers were not willing to entrust the power even to the President and the Senators, and it was therefore expressly provided that only Congress could take this momentous step.

Here, again, the theory of the Constitution was necessarily somewhat modified in practical administration, for under the power of nominating diplomatic representatives, negotiating treaties, and in general, of executing the laws of the nation, the principle was soon evolved that the conduct of foreign affairs was primarily the function of the President, with the limitation that the Senate must concur in diplomatic appointments and in the validity of treaties, and that only both Houses of Congress could jointly declare war. This cumbrous system necessarily required that the President in conducting the foreign relations of the Government should keep in touch with the Senate, and such was the accepted procedure throughout the history of the nation until President Wilson saw fit to ignore the Senate, even when the Senate had indicated its dissent in advance to some of his policies at the Versailles Conference.

I suppose that since that conference no part of our constitutional system has caused more adverse comment in Europe than this system. It often handicaps the United States from taking a speedy and effectual part in international negotiations, although if the President and the Senate be in harmony and collaborate in this joint responsibility, there is no necessary reason why this should be so.

I share the view of many Americans that this provision of the Constitution was wise and salutary, especially at this time, when the United States has taken such an important position in the councils of civilization. The President is a very powerful Executive, and his tenure, while short, is fixed. Generally he is elected by little more than a majority of the people, and sometimes through the curious workings of the electoral college system, he has been only the choice of a minority of the electorate. For these reasons, the framers of the Constitution were unwilling to vest in the President exclusively the immeasurable power of pledging the faith, man-power, and resources of the nation and of declaring war. The heterogeneous character of our population especially emphasizes the wisdom of this course, for it would be difficult, if not impossible, for an American President to make an offensive and defensive alliance with any nation or declare war against another nation without running counter to the racial interests and passions of a substantial part of the American nation. For better or worse, the United States has limited, but not destroyed, as the world war showed, its freedom to antagonize powerful nations from whose people it has drawn large numbers of its own citizenship. The domestic harmony of the nation requires that before the United States assumes treaty obligations or makes war such policy shall represent the largely preponderating sentiment of its people, and nothing could more effectually secure this end than to require the President, before making a treaty, to secure the assent of two-thirds of the Senate and a majority of both Houses of Congress before making war.

While this may lead, as it has in recent years, to temporary and regrettable embarrassments, yet in the long run, it is not only better for the United States, but it is even to the best interests of other nations, for in this way they are safeguarded against the possible action of an Executive with whom racial instincts might still be very influential. In your country, where the Government of the day is subject to immediate dismissal for want of confidence, such power over foreign relations can be safely entrusted to a few men, but in the United States, with its fixed tenures of office, a President could pledge the faith and involve his nation in war against the interests and will of the people. Suppose the President had unlimited power over our foreign relations and that within the next ten years an American, whose parents were born in any European nation, was elected on purely domestic issues, he could, with his assured four years of power, bring about a new alignment of nations and shake the political equilibrium of the world. The Constitution wisely refused to grant such a power. Hence the provision for the concurrence of the legislative representatives of the nation. At all events, it constitutes a system which, as the last presidential election showed, the American people will not willingly forgo. It is true that this system makes it difficult for the United States to participate effectively in the main purpose of the League of Nations to enforce peace by joint action at Geneva, but to ask the United States to surrender a vital part of its constitutional system, upon which its domestic peace so largely depends, in order to promote the League, seems to me as unreasonable as it would be to ask your country to abolish the Crown, to which it is sincerely attached as a vital part of its system, as a contribution towards international co-operation. You would not surrender such an integral part of your system, and therefore it is not reasonable to expect a similar sacrifice on our part, even though the meritorious purposes of the League be freely recognized.

I have thus summarized briefly and most inadequately some of the essential principles of the Constitution. I have only been able to suggest very impressionistically what they are and the lessons to be drawn from them. If I were able to deliver a dozen addresses on the subject in this historic Hall and with this indulgent audience I would not scratch even the surface. To understand the Constitution of the United States you must not only read the text but the thousands of opinions rendered in the last 130 years by the Supreme Court in its great task of interpreting this wonderful document. Few documents have been the subject of more extended commentaries. The four thousand words have been meticulously examined through intellectual microscopes in judicial opinions, textbooks, and other commentaries which are as "thick as autumnal leaves that strow the brooks in Vallombrosa."

One can say of this document as Dr. Furness, in his variorum edition of Hamlet, says of the words of that character:

"No words by him let fall, no syllable by him uttered, but has been caught up and pondered, as no words except those of Holy Writ."

But what of its future and how long will the Constitution wholly resist the washing of time and circumstance? Lord Macaulay once ventured the prediction that the Constitution would prove unworkable as soon as there were no longer large areas of undeveloped land and when the United States became a nation of great cities. That period of development has arrived. In 1880 only 15 per cent. of the American population lived in the cities and the remainder were still on the farms. To-day over 52 per cent, are crowded in one hundred great cities. Lord Macaulay added:

"I believe America's fate is only deferred by physical causes. Institutions purely democratic will sooner or later destroy liberty or civilization, or both…. The American Constitution is all sail and no anchor."

In this last commentary Lord Macaulay was clearly mistaken. As I have shown, the Constitution is not "purely democratic." It is amazing that so great a mind should have so little understood that more than any other Constitution, that of America imposes powerful restraints on democracy. The experience of a century and a quarter has shown that while the anchor may at times drag, yet it measurably holds the ship of state to its ancient moorings. The American Constitution still remains in its essential principles and still enjoys not only the confidence but the affection of the great and varied people whom it rules. To the latter this remarkable achievement must be attributed rather than to any inherent strength in parchment or red seals, for in a democracy the living soul of any Constitution must be such belief of the people in its wisdom and justice. If it should perish to-morrow, it would yet have enjoyed a life and growth of which any nation or age might be justly proud. Moreover, it could claim with truth, if it finally perished, that it had been subjected to conditions for which it was never intended and that some of its essential principles had been ignored.

The Constitution is something more than a written formula of government—it is a great spirit. It is a high and noble assertion, and, indeed, vindication, of the morality of government. It "renders unto Caesar [the political state] the things that are Caesar's," but in safeguarding the fundamental moral rights of the people, it "renders unto God the things that are God's."

In concluding, I cannot refrain from again reminding you that this consummate work of statecraft was the work of the English-speaking race, and that your people can therefore justly share in the pride which it awakens. It is not only one of the great achievements of that gens aeterna, but also one of the great monuments of human progress. It illustrates the possibilities of true democracy in its best estate. When the moral anarchy out of which it was born is called to mind, it can be truly said that while "sown in weakness, it was raised in power."

To the succeeding ages, it will be a flaming beacon, and everywhere men, who are confronted with the acute problems of this complex age, can take encouragement from the fact that a small and weak people, when confronted with similar problems, had the strength and will to impose restraint upon themselves by peacefully proclaiming in the simple words of the noble preamble to the Constitution:

"We, the people of the United States, in order to form a more perfect union, establish justice, ensure domestic tranquillity, provide for the common defence, promote the general welfare, and secure the blessings of liberty to ourselves and our posterity, do ordain and establish this Constitution for the United States of America."

Note the words "ordain and establish." They imply perpetuity. They make no provision for the secession of any State, even if it deems itself aggrieved by federal action. And yet the right to secede was urged for many years, but Lincoln completed the work of Washington, Franklin, Madison and Hamilton by establishing that "a government for the people, by the people and of the people should not perish from the earth."

IV. The Revolt Against Authority

"Where there is no vision, the people perish: but he that keepeth the law, happy is he."

PROVERBS xxix. 18.

One of the most quoted—and also mis-quoted—proverbs of the wise Solomon says, as translated in the authorized version: "Where there is no vision, the people perish." What Solomon actually said was: "Where there is no vision, the people cast off restraint." The translator thus confused an effect with a cause. What was the vision to which the Wise Man referred? The rest of the proverb, which is rarely quoted, explains:

"Where there is no vision, the people cast off restraint: but he that keepeth the law, happy is he."

The vision, then, is the authority of law, and Solomon's warning is that to which the great and noble founder of Pennsylvania, William Penn, many centuries later gave utterance, when he said:

"That government is free to the people under it, where the laws rule and the people are a party to those laws; and all the rest is tyranny, oligarchy and confusion."

It is my present purpose to discuss the moral psychology of the present revolt against the spirit of authority. Too little consideration has been paid by the legal profession to questions of moral psychology. These have been left to metaphysicians and ecclesiastics, and yet—to paraphrase the saying of the Master—"the laws were made for man and not man for the laws," and if the science of the law ignores the study of human nature and attempts to conform man to the laws, rather than the laws to man, then its development is a very partial and imperfect one.

Let me first be sure of my premises. Is there in this day and generation a spirit of lawlessness greater or different than that that has always characterized human society? Such spirit of revolt against authority has always existed, even when the penalty of death was visited upon nearly all offences against life and property. Blackstone tells us (Book IV, Chap. I) that in the eighteenth century it was a capital offence to cut down a cherry tree in an orchard—a drastic penalty which should increase our admiration for George Washington's courage and veracity.

We are apt to see the past in a golden haze, which obscures our vision. Thus, we think of William Penn's "holy experiment" on the banks of the Delaware as the realization of Sir Thomas More's dream of Utopia; and yet Pennsylvania was somewhat intemperately called in 1698 "the greatest refuge for pirates and rogues in America," and Penn himself wrote, about that time, that he had heard of no place which was "more overrun with wickedness" than his City of Brotherly Love, where things were so "openly committed in defiance of law and virtue—facts so foul that I am forbid by common modesty to relate them."

Conceding that lawlessness is not a novel phenomenon, is not the present time characterized by an exceptional revolt against the authority of law? The statistics of our criminal courts show in recent years an unprecedented growth in crimes. Thus, in the federal courts, pending criminal indictments have increased from 9503 in the year 1912 to over 70,000 in the year 1921. While this abnormal increase is, in part, due to sumptuary legislation—for approximately 30,000 cases now pending arise under the prohibition statutes—yet, eliminating these, there yet remains an increase in nine years of over 400 per cent, in the comparatively narrow sphere of the federal criminal jurisdiction. I have been unable to get the data from the State Courts; but the growth of crimes can be measured by a few illustrative statistics. Thus, the losses from burglaries which have been repaid by casualty companies have grown in amount from $886,000 in 1914 to over $10,000,000 in 1920; and, in a like period, embezzlements have increased five-fold. It is notorious that the thefts from the mails and express companies and other carriers have grown to enormous proportions. The hold-up of railroad trains is now of frequent occurrence, and is not confined to the unsettled sections of the country. Not only in the United States, but even in Europe, such crimes of violence are of increasing frequency, and a recent dispatch from Berne, under date of August 7, 1921, stated that the famous International Expresses of Europe were now run under a military guard.

The streets of our cities, once reasonably secure from crimes of violence, have now become the field of operations for the foot-pad and highwayman. The days of Dick Turpin and Jack Sheppard have returned, with this serious difference—that the Turpins and Sheppards of our day are not dependent upon the horse, but have the powerful automobile to facilitate their crimes and make sure their escape.

Thus in Chicago alone, 5000 automobiles were stolen in a single year. Once murder was an infrequent and abnormal crime. To-day in our large cities it is of almost daily occurrence. In New York, in 1917, there were 236 murders and only 67 convictions; in 1918, 221, and 77 convictions. In Chicago, in 1919, there were 336, and 44 convictions.

When the crime wave was at its height a year ago, the police authorities in more than one American city confessed their impotence to impose effective restraints. Life and property had seemingly become almost as insecure as during the Middle Ages.[3]

[Footnote 3: The reader will bear in mind that these words were spoken in August 1921. Unquestionably, the situation has greatly improved during the present year(1922).]

As to the subtler and more insidious crimes against the political state, it is enough to say that graft has become a science in city, state and nation. Losses by such misapplication of public funds—piled Pelion on Ossa—no longer run in the millions but the hundreds of millions. Our city governments are, in many instances, foul cancers on the body politic; and for us to boast of having solved the problem of local self-government is as fatuous as for a strong man to exult in his health when his body is covered with running sores. It has been estimated that the annual profits from violations of the prohibition laws have reached $300,000,000. Men who thus violate these laws for sordid gain are not likely to obey other laws, and the respect for law among all classes steadily diminishes as our people become familiar with, and tolerant to, wholesale criminality. Whether the moral and economic results of Prohibition overbalance this rising wave of crime, time will tell.

In limine, let us note the significant fact that this spirit of revolt against authority is not confined to the political state, and therefore its causes lie beyond that sphere of human action.

Human life is governed by all manner of man-made laws—laws of art, of social intercourse, of literature, music, business—all evolved by custom and imposed by the collective will of society. Here we find the same revolt against tradition and authority.

In music, its fundamental canons have been thrown aside and discord has been substituted for harmony as its ideal. Its culmination—jazz—is a musical crime. If the forms of dancing and music are symptomatic of an age, what shall be said of the universal craze to indulge in crude and clumsy dancing to the vile discords of so-called "jazz" music? The cry of the time is:

"On with the dance, let joy be" unrefined.

In the plastic arts, the laws of form and the criteria of beauty have been swept aside by the futurists, cubists, vorticists, tactilists, and other aesthetic Bolsheviki.

In poetry, where beauty of rhythm, melody of sound and nobility of thought were once regarded as the true tests, we now have in freak forms of poetry the exaltation of the grotesque and brutal. Hundreds of poets are feebly echoing the "barbaric yawp" of Walt Whitman, without the redeeming merit of his occasional sublimity of thought.

In commerce, the revolt is against the purity of standards and the integrity of business morals. Who can question that this is pre-eminently the age of the sham and the counterfeit? Science is prostituted to deceive the public by cloaking the increasing deterioration in quality of merchandise. The blatant medium of advertising has become so mendacious as to defeat its own purpose.

In the recent deflation in commodity values, there was widespread "welching" among business men who had theretofore been classed as reputable. Of course, I recognize that a far greater number kept their contracts, even when it brought them to the verge of ruin. But when in the history of American business was there such a volume of broken faith as in the drastic deflation of 1920?

In the greater sphere of social life, we find the same revolt against the institutions which have the sanction of the past. Social laws, which mark the decent restraints of print, speech and dress, have in recent decades been increasingly disregarded. The very foundations of the great and primitive institutions of mankind—like the family, the Church, and the State—have been shaken. Nature itself is defied. Thus, the fundamental difference of sex is disregarded by social and political movements which ignore the permanent differentiation of social function ordained by Nature.

All these are but illustrations of the general revolt against the authority of the past—a revolt that can be measured by the change in the fundamental presumption of men with respect to the value of human experience. In all former ages, all that was in the past was presumptively true, and the burden was upon him who sought to change it. To-day, the human mind apparently regards the lessons of the past as presumptively false—and the burden is upon him who seeks to invoke them.

Lest I be accused of undue pessimism, let me cite as a witness one who, of all men, is probably best equipped to express an opinion upon the moral state of the world. I refer to the venerable head of that religious organization[4] which, with its trained representatives in every part of the world, is probably better informed as to its spiritual state than any other organization.

[Footnote 4: Reference is to the late Pope Benedict.]

Speaking last Christmas Eve, in an address to the College of Cardinals, the venerable Pontiff gave expression to an estimate of present conditions which should have attracted far greater attention than it apparently did. The Pope said that five plagues were now afflicting humanity.

The first was the unprecedented challenge to authority.

The second, an equally unprecedented hatred between man and man.

The third was the abnormal aversion to work.

The fourth, the excessive thirst for pleasure as the great aim of life.

The fifth, a gross materialism which denied the reality of the spiritual in human life.

The accuracy of this indictment will commend itself to men who like myself are not of Pope Benedict's communion.

I trust that I have already shown that the challenge to authority is universal and is not confined to that of the political state. Even in the narrower confine of the latter, the fires of revolution are either violently burning, or, at least, smouldering. Two of the oldest empires in the world, which, together, have more than half of its population (China and Russia) are in a welter of anarchy; while many lesser nations are in a stage of submerged revolt. If the revolt were confined to autocratic governments, we might see in it merely a reaction against tyranny; but even in the most stable of democracies and among the most enlightened peoples, the underground rumblings of revolution may be heard.

The Government of Italy has been preserved from overthrow, not alone by its constituted authorities, but by a band of resolute men, called the "fascisti," who have taken the law into their own hands, as did the vigilance committees in western mining camps, to put down worse disorders.

Even England, the mother of democracies, and the most stable of all Governments in the maintenance of law, has been shaken to its very foundations in the last three years, when powerful groups of men attempted to seize the State by the throat and compel submission to their demands by threatening to starve the community. This would be serious enough if it were only the world-old struggle between capital and labour and had only involved the conditions of manual toil. But the insurrection against the political state in England was more political than it was economic. It marked, on the part of millions of men, a portentous decay of belief in representative government and its chosen organ—the ballot box. Great and powerful groups had suddenly discovered—and it may be the most portentous political discovery of the twentieth century—that the power involved in their control over the necessaries of life, as compared with the power of the voting franchise, was as a forty-two centimetre cannon to the bow and arrow. The end sought to be attained, namely the nationalization of the basic industries, and even the control of the foreign policy of Great Britain, vindicated the truth of the British Prime Minister's statement that these great strikes involved something more than a mere struggle over the conditions of labour, and that they were essentially seditious attempts against the life of the State.[5]

[Footnote 5: I am here speaking of the conditions of 1920. I appreciate the great improvement, which seems to me to justify the Lincoln-like patience of Lloyd George.]

Nor were they altogether unsuccessful; for, when the armies of Lenin and Trotsky were at the gates of Warsaw, in the summer of 1920, the attempts of the Governments of England and Belgium to afford assistance to the embattled Poles were paralysed by the labour groups of both countries, who threatened a general strike if those two nations joined with France in aiding Poland to resist a possibly greater menace to Western civilization than has occurred since Attila and his Huns stood on the banks of the Marne.

Of greater significance to the welfare of civilization is the complete subversion during the world war of nearly all the international laws which had been slowly built up in a thousand years. These principles, as codified by the two Hague Conventions, were immediately swept aside in the fierce struggle for existence, and civilized man, with his liquid fire and poison gas and his deliberate; attacks upon undefended cities and their women and children, waged war with the unrelenting ferocity of primitive times.

Surely, this fierce war of extermination, which caused the loss of three hundred billion dollars in property and thirty millions of human lives, did mark for the time being the "twilight of civilization." The hands on the dial of time had been put back—temporarily, let us hope and pray—a thousand years.

Nor will many question the accuracy of the second count in Pope Benedict's indictment. The war to end war only ended in unprecedented hatred between nation and nation, class and class, and man and man. Victors and vanquished are involved in a common ruin. And if in this deluge of blood, which has submerged the world, there is a Mount Ararat, upon which the ark of a truer and better peace can find refuge, it has not yet appeared above the troubled surface of the waters.

Still less can one question the closely related third and fourth counts in Pope Benedict's indictment, namely the unprecedented aversion to work, when work is most needed to reconstruct the foundations of prosperity, or the excessive thirst for pleasure which preceded, accompanied, and now has followed the most terrible tragedy in the annals of mankind. The true spirit of work seems to have vanished from millions of men; that spirit of which Shakespeare made his Orlando speak when he said of his true servant, Adam:

"O good old man! how well in thee appears
The constant service of the antique world.
When service sweat for duty, not for meed!"

The moral of our industrial civilization has been shattered. Work for work's sake, as the most glorious privilege of human faculties, has gone, both as an ideal and as a potent spirit. The conception of work as a degrading servitude, to be done with reluctance and grudging inefficiency, seems to be the ideal of millions of men of all classes and in all countries.

The spirit of work is of more than sentimental importance. It may be said of it, as Hamlet says of death: "The readiness is all." All of us are conscious of the fact that, given a love of work, and the capacity for it seems almost illimitable—as witness Napoleon, with his thousand-man power, or Shakespeare, who in twenty years could write more than twenty masterpieces.

On the other hand, given an aversion to work, and the less a man does the less he wants to do, or is seemingly capable of doing.

The great evil of the world to-day is this aversion to work. As the mechanical era diminished the element of physical exertion in work, we would have supposed that man would have sought expression for his physical faculties in other ways. On the contrary, the whole history of the mechanical era is a persistent struggle for more pay and less work, and to-day it has culminated in world-wide ruin; for there is not a nation in civilization which is not now in the throes of economic distress, and many of them are on the verge of ruin. In my judgment, the economic catastrophe of 1921 is far greater than the politico-military catastrophe of 1914.

The results of these two tendencies, measured in the statistics of productive industry, are literally appalling.

Thus, in 1920, Italy, according to statistics of her Minister of Labour, lost 55,000,000 days of work because of strikes alone. From July to September, many great factories were in the hands of revolutionary communists. A full third of these strikes had for their end political and not economic purposes.

In Germany, the progressive revolt of labour against work is thus measured by competent authority: There were lost in strikes in 1917, 900,000 working days; in 1918, 4,900,000, and, in 1919, 46,600,000.

Even in our own favoured land, the same phenomena are observable. In the State of New York alone for 1920, there was a loss due to strikes of over 10,000,000 working days.

In all countries the losses by such cessations from labour are little as compared with those due to the spirit which in England is called "ca'-canny" or the shirking of performance of work, and of sabotage, which means the deliberate destruction of machinery in operation. Everywhere the phenomenon has been observed that, with the highest wages known in the history of modern times, there has been an unmistakable lessening of efficiency, and that with an increase in the number of workers, there has been a decrease in output. Thus, the transportation companies in the United States have seriously made a claim against the United States

Government for damages to their roads, amounting to $750,000,000, claimed to be due to the inefficiency of labour during the period of governmental operation.

Accompanying this indisposition to work efficiently has been a mad desire for pleasure, such as, if it existed in like measure in preceding ages, has not been seen within the memory of living man. Man has danced upon the verge of a social abyss, and, as previously suggested, the dancing has, both in form and in accompanying music, lost its former grace and reverted to the primitive forms of crude vulgarity.

which gives the spectators the maximum of emotional expression with the minimum of mental effort, had not been eclipsed by the splendour of a Dempsey or a Carpentier.

Of the last count in Pope Benedict's indictment, I shall say but little. It is more appropriate for the members of that great and noble profession which is more intimately concerned with the spiritual advance of mankind. It is enough to say that, while the Church as an institution continues to exist, the belief in the supernatural and even in the spiritual has been supplanted in the souls of millions of men by a gross and debasing materialism.

If my reader agrees with me in my premises then we are not likely to disagree in the conclusion that the causes of these grave symptoms are not ephemeral or superficial; but must have their origin in some deep-seated and world-wide change in human society. If there is to be a remedy, we must first diagnose this malady of the human soul.

For example, let us not "lay the flattering unction to our souls" that this spirit is solely the reaction of the great war.

The present weariness and lassitude of human spirit and the disappointment and disillusion as to the aftermath of the harvest of blood, may have aggravated, but they could not cause the symptoms of which I speak; for the very obvious reason that all these symptoms were in existence and apparent to a few discerning men for decades before the war. Indeed, it is possible that the world war, far from causing the malaise of the age, was, in itself, but one of its many symptoms.

Undoubtedly, there are many contributing causes which have swollen the turbid tide of this world-wide revolution against the spirit of authority.

Thus, the multiplicity of laws does not tend to develop a law-abiding spirit. This fact has often been noted. Thus Napoleon, on the eve of the 18th Brumaire, complained that France, with a thousand folios of law, was a lawless nation. Unquestionably, the political state suffers in authority by the abuse of legislation, and especially by the appeal to law to curb evils that are best left to individual conscience.

In this age of democracy, the average individual is too apt to recognize two constitutions—one, the constitution of the State, and the second, an unwritten constitution, to him of higher authority, under which he believes that no law is obligatory which he regards as in excess of the true powers of government. Of this latter spirit, the widespread violation of the prohibition law is a familiar illustration.

A race of individualists obey reluctantly, when they obey at all, any laws which they regard as unreasonable or vexatious. Indeed, they are increasingly opposed to any law, which affects their selfish interests. Thus many good women are involuntary smugglers. They deny the authority of the state to impose a tax upon a Paquin gown. The law's delays and laxity in administration breed a spirit of contempt, and too often invite men to take the law into their own hands. These causes are so familiar that their statement is a commonplace.

Proceeding to deeper and less recognized causes, some would attribute this spirit of lawlessness to the rampant individualism, which began in the eighteenth century, and which has steadily and naturally grown with the advance of democratic institutions. Undoubtedly, the excessive emphasis upon the rights of man, which marked the political upheaval of the close of the eighteenth and the beginning of the nineteenth century, has contributed to this malady of the age. Men talked, and still talk, loudly of their rights, but too rarely of their duties. And yet if we were to attribute the malady merely to excessive individualism, we would again err in mistaking a symptom for a cause.

To diagnose truly this malady we must look to some cause that is coterminous in time with the disease itself and which has been operative throughout civilization. We must seek some widespread change in social conditions, for man's essential nature has changed but little, and the change must, therefore, be of environment.

I know of but one such change that is sufficiently widespread and deep-seated to account adequately for this malady of our time.

Beginning with the close of the eighteenth century, and continuing throughout the nineteenth, a prodigious transformation has taken place in the environment of man, which has done more to revolutionize the conditions of human life than all the changes that had taken place in the 500,000 preceding years which science has attributed to man's life on the planet. Up to the period of Watt's discovery of steam vapour as a motive power, these conditions, so far as the principal facilities of life, were substantially those of the civilization which developed eighty centuries ago on the banks of the Nile and later on the Euphrates. Man had indeed increased his conquest over Nature in later centuries by a few mechanical inventions, such as gunpowder, telescope, magnetic needle, printing-press, spinning jenny, and hand-loom, but the characteristic of all those inventions, with the exception of gunpowder, was that they still remained a subordinate auxiliary to the physical strength and mental skill of man. In other words, man still dominated the machine, and there was still full play for his physical and mental faculties. Moreover, all the inventions of preceding ages, from the first fashioning of the flint to the spinning-wheel and the hand-lever press, were all conquests of the tangible and visible forces of Nature.

With Watt's utilization of steam vapour as a motive power, man suddenly passed into a new and portentous chapter of his varied history. Thenceforth, he was to multiply his powers a thousandfold by the utilization of the invisible powers of Nature—such as vapour and electricity. This prodigious change in his powers, and therefore his environment, has proceeded with ever-accelerating speed.

Man has suddenly become the superman. Like the giants of the ancient fable, he has stormed the very ramparts of Divine power, or, like Prometheus, he has stolen fire of omnipotent forces from Heaven itself for his use. His voice can now reach from the Atlantic to the Pacific, and, taking wing in his aeroplane, he can fly in one swift flight from Nova Scotia to England, or he can leave Lausanne and, resting upon the icy summit of Mont Blanc—thus, like "the herald, Mercury, new-lighted on a heaven-kissing hill"—he can again plunge into the void, and thus outfly the eagles themselves.

In thus acquiring from the forces of Nature almost illimitable power, he has minimized the necessity for his own physical exertion or even mental skill. The machine now not only acts for him, but too often thinks for him.

Is it surprising that so portentous a change should have fevered his brain and disturbed his mental equilibrium? A new ideal, which he proudly called "progress," obsessed him, the ideal of quantity and not quality. His practical religion became that of acceleration and facilitation—to do things more quickly and easily—and thus to minimize exertion became his great objective. Less and less he relied upon the initiative of his own brain and muscle, and more and more he put his faith in the power of machinery to relieve him of labour. The evil of our age is that its values are all false. It overrates speed, it underrates sureness; it overrates the new, it underrates the old; it overrates automatic efficiency, it underrates individual craftsmanship; it overrates rights, it underrates duties; it overrates political institutions, it underrates individual responsibility. We glory in the fact that we can talk a thousand miles, but we ignore the greater question, whether when we thus out-do Stentor, we have anything worth saying. We have now made the serene spaces of the upper Heavens our media to transmit market reports and sporting news, second-rate music and worse oratory and in the meantime the great masters of thought, Homer and Shakespeare, Bach and Beethoven remain unbidden on our library shelves. What a sordid Vanity Fair is our modern Civilization!

This incalculable multiplication of power has intoxicated man. The lust has obsessed him, without regard to whether it be constructive or destructive.

Quantity, not quality, becomes the great objective. Man consumes the treasures of the earth faster than he produces them, deforesting its surface and disembowelling its hidden wealth. As he feverishly multiplied the things he desired, even more feverishly he multiplied his wants.

To gain these, man sought the congested centres of human life. While the world, as a whole, is not over-populated, the leading countries of civilization were subjected to this tremendous pressure. Europe, which, at the beginning of the nineteenth century, barely numbered 100,000,000 people, suddenly grew nearly five-fold. Millions left the farms to gather into the cities to exploit their new and seemingly easy conquest over Nature.

In the United States, as recently as 1880, only 15 per cent. of the people were crowded in the cities, 85 per cent. remained upon the farms and still followed that occupation, which, of all occupations, still preserves, in its integrity, the dominance of human labour over the machine. To-day, 52 per cent. of the population is in the cities, and with many of them existence is both feverish and artificial. While they have employment, many of them do not themselves work, but spend their lives in watching machines work.

The result has been a minute subdivision of labour that has denied to many workers the true significance and physical benefit of labour.

The direct results of this excessive tendency to specialization, whereby not only the work but the worker becomes divided into mere fragments, are threefold. Hobson, in his work on John Ruskin, thus classifies them. In the first place, narrowness, due to the confinement to a single action in which the elements of human skill or strength are largely eliminated; secondly, monotony, in the assimilation of man to a machine, whereby seemingly the machine dominates man and not man the machine, and, thirdly, irrationality, in that work became dissociated in the mind of the worker with any complete or satisfying achievement. The worker does not see the fruit of his travail, and cannot therefore be truly satisfied. To spend one's life in opening a valve to make a part of a pin is, as Ruskin pointed out, demoralizing in its tendencies. The clerk who only operates an adding machine has little opportunity for self-expression.

Thus, millions of men have lost both the opportunity for real physical exertion, the incentive to work in the joyous competition of skill, and finally the reward of work in the sense of achievement.

More serious than this, however, has been the destructive effort of quantity, the great object of the mechanical age, at the expense of quality.

Take, for example, the printing-press: No one can question the immense advantages which have flowed from the increased facility for transmitting ideas. But may it not be true that the thousandfold increase in such transmission by the rotary press has also tended to muddy the current thought of the time? True it is that the printing-press has piled up great treasures of human knowledge which make this age the richest in accessible information. I am not speaking of knowledge, but rather of the current thought of the living generation.

I gravely question whether it has the same clarity as the brain of the generation which fashioned the Constitution of the United States. Our fathers could not talk over the telephone for three thousand miles, but have we surpassed them in thoughts of enduring value? Washington and Franklin could not travel sixty miles an hour in a railroad train, or twice that speed in an aeroplane, but does it follow that they did not travel to as good purpose as we, who scurry to and fro like the ants in a disordered ant-heap? Unquestionably, man of to-day has a thousand ideas suggested to him by the newspaper and the library where our ancestors had one; but have we the same spirit of calm inquiry and do we co-ordinate the facts we know as wisely as our ancestors did?

Athens in the days of Pericles had but thirty thousand people and few mechanical inventions; but she produced philosophers, poets and artists, whose work after more than twenty centuries still remain the despair of the would-be imitators.

Shakespeare had a theatre with the ground as its floor and the sky as its ceiling; but New York, which has fifty theatres and annually spends $100,000,000 in the box offices of its varied amusement resorts, has rarely in two centuries produced a play that has lived.

To-day, man has a cinematographic brain. A thousand images are impressed daily upon the screen of his consciousness, but they are as fleeting as moving pictures in a cinema theatre. The American Press prints every year over 29,000,000,000 issues. No one can question its educational possibilities, for the best of all colleges is potentially the University of Gutenberg. If it printed only the truth, its value would be infinite; but who can say in what proportions of this vast volume of printed matter is the true and the false? The framers of the Constitution had few books and fewer newspapers. Their thoughts were few and simple, but what they lacked in quantity they made up in unsurpassed quality.

Before the beginning of the present mechanical age, the current of living thought could be likened to a mountain stream, which though confined within narrow banks yet had waters of transparent clearness. May not the current thought of our time be compared with the mighty Mississippi in the period of a spring freshet? Its banks are wide and its current is swift, but the turbid stream that flows onward is one of muddy swirls and eddies and overflows its banks to their destruction.

The great indictment, however, of the present age of mechanical power is that it has largely destroyed the spirit of work. The great enigma which it propounds to us, and which, like the riddle of the Sphinx, we will solve or be destroyed, is this:

Has the increase in the potential of human power, through

thermodynamics, been accompanied by a corresponding increase in the potential of human character?

To this life and death question, a great French philosopher, Le Bon, writing in 1910, replied that the one unmistakable symptom of human life was "the increasing deterioration in human character," and a great physicist has described the symptom as "the progressive enfeeblement of the human will."

In a famous book, Degeneration, written at the close of the nineteenth century, Max Nordau, as a pathologist, explains this tendency by arguing that our complex civilization has placed too great a strain upon the limited nervous organization of man.

A great financier, the elder J.P. Morgan, once said of an existing financial condition that it was suffering from "undigested securities," and, paraphrasing him, is it not possible that man is suffering from undigested achievements and that his salvation must lie in adaptation to a new environment, which, measured by any standard known to science, is a thousandfold greater in this year of grace than it was at the beginning of the nineteenth century?

No one would be mad enough to urge such a retrogression as the abandonment of labour-saving machinery would involve. Indeed, it would be impossible; for, in speaking of its evils, I freely recognize that not only would civilization perish without its beneficent aid, but that every step forward in the history of man has been coincident with, and in large part attributable to, a new mechanical invention.

But suppose the development of labour-saving machinery should reach a stage where all human labour was eliminated, what would be the effect on man? The answer is contained in an experiment which Sir John Lubbock made with a tribe of ants. Originally the most voracious and militant of their species, yet when denied the opportunity for exercise and freed from the necessity of foraging for their food, in three generations they became anaemic and perished.

Take from man the opportunity of work and the sense of pride in achievement and you have taken from him the very life of his existence. Robert Burns could sing as he drove his ploughshare through the fields of Ayr. To-day millions who simply watch an automatic infallible machine, which requires neither strength nor skill, do not sing at their work but too many curse the fate, which has chained them, like Ixion, to a soulless machine.

The evil is even greater.

The specialization of our modern mechanical civilization has caused a submergence of the individual into the group or class. Man is fast ceasing to be the unit of human society. Self-governing groups are becoming the new units. This is true of all classes of men, the employer as well as the employee. The true justification for the American anti-monopoly statutes, including the Sherman anti-trust law, lies not so much in the realm of economics as in that of morals. With the submergence of the individual, whether he be capitalist or wage-earner, into a group, there has followed the dissipation of moral responsibility. A mass morality has been substituted for individual morality, and unfortunately, group morality generally intensifies the vices more than the virtues of man.

Possibly, the greatest result of the mechanical age is this spirit of organization.

Its merits are manifold and do not require statement; but they have blinded us to the demerits of excessive organization.

We are now beginning to see—slowly, but surely—that a faculty of organization which, as such, submerged the spirit of individualism, is not an unmixed good.

Indeed, the moral lesson of the tragedy of Germany is the demoralizing influence of organization carried to the _n_th power. No nation was ever more highly organized than this modern State. Physically, intellectually and spiritually it had become a highly developed machine. Its dominating mechanical spirit so submerged the individual that, in 1914, the paradox was observed of an enlightened nation that was seemingly destitute of a conscience.

What was true of Germany, however, was true—although in lesser degree—of all civilized nations. In all of them, the individual had been submerged in group formations, and the effect upon the character of man has been destructive of his nobler self.

This may explain the paradox of so-called "progress." It may be likened to a great wheel, which, from the increasing domination of mechanical forces, developed an ever-accelerating speed, until, by centrifugal action, it went off its bearings in 1914 and caused an unprecedented catastrophe. As man slowly pulls himself out of that gigantic wreck and recovers consciousness, he begins to realize that speed is not necessarily progress.

Of all this, the nineteenth century, in its exultant pride in its conquest of the invisible forces, was almost blind. It not only accepted progress as an unmistakable fact—mistaking, however, acceleration and facilitation for progress—but in its mad folly believed in an immutable law of progress which, working with the blind forces of machinery, would propel man forward.

A few men, however, standing on the mountain ranges of human observation, saw the future more clearly than did the mass. Emerson, Carlyle, Ruskin, Samuel Butler, and Max Nordau, in the nineteenth century, and, in our time, Ferrero, all pointed out the inevitable dangers of the excessive mechanization of human society. The prophecies were unhappily as little heeded as those of Cassandra.

One can see the tragedy of the time, as a few saw it, in comparing the first Locksley Hall of Alfred Tennyson, written in 1827, with its abiding faith in the "increasing purpose of the ages" and its roseate prophecies of the golden age, when the "war-drum would throb no longer and the battle flags be furled in the Parliament of Man and the Federation of the World," and the later Locksley Hall, written sixty years later, when the great spiritual poet of our time gave utterance to the dark pessimism which flooded his soul:

"Gone the cry of 'Forward, Forward,' lost within a growing gloom;
Lost, or only heard in silence from the silence of a tomb.
Half the marvels of my morning, triumphs over time and space,
Staled by frequence, shrunk by usage, into commonest commonplace!
Evolution ever climbing after some ideal good,
And Reversion ever dragging Evolution in the mud.
Is it well that while we range with Science, glorying in the Time,
City children soak and blacken soul and sense in city slime?"

Am I unduly pessimistic? I fear that this is the case with most men who, like Dante, have crossed their fiftieth year and find themselves in a "dark and sombre wood."

My reader will probably subject me to the additional reproach that I suggest no remedy.

There are many palliatives for the evils which I have discussed. To rekindle in men the love of work for work's sake and the spirit of discipline, which the lost sense of human solidarity once inspired, would do much to solve the problem, for work is the greatest moral force in the world. But I must frankly add that I have neither the time nor the qualifications to discuss the solution of this grave problem.

If we of this generation can only recognize that the evil exists, then the situation is not past remedy; for man has never yet found himself in a blind alley of negation. He is still "master of his soul and captain of his fate," and, to me, the most encouraging sign of the times is the persistent evidence of contemporary literature that thoughtful men now recognize that much of our boasted progress was as unreal as a rainbow. While the temper of the times seems for the moment pessimistic, it merely marks the recognition of man of an abyss whose existence he barely suspected but over which his indomitable courage will yet carry him.

I have faith in the inextinguishable spark of the Divine, which is in the human soul and which our complex mechanical civilization has not extinguished. Of this, the world war was in itself a proof. All the horrible resources of mechanics and chemistry were utilized to coerce the human soul, and all proved ineffectual. Never did men rise to greater heights of self-sacrifice or show a greater fidelity "even unto death." Millions went to their graves, as to their beds, for an ideal; and when that is possible, this

Pandora's box of modern civilization, which contained all imaginable evils, as well as benefits, also leaves hope behind.

I am reminded of a remark that the great Roumanian statesman, Taku Jonescu, made during the Peace Conference at Paris. When asked his views as to the future of civilization, he replied: "Judged by the light of reason there is but little hope, but I have faith in man's inextinguishable impulse to live."

Happily, that cannot be affected by any change in man's environment! For even when the cave-man retreated from the advance of the polar cap, which once covered Europe with Arctic desolation, he not only defied the elements but showed even then the love of the sublime by beautifying the walls of his icy prison with those mural decorations which were the beginning of art.

Assuredly, the man of to-day, with the rich heritage of countless ages, can do no less. He has but to diagnose the evil and he will then, in some way, meet it.

But what can man-made law do in this warfare against the blind forces of Nature?

It is easy to exaggerate the value of all political institutions; for they are generally on the surface of human life and do not reach down to the deep under-currents of human nature. But the law can do something to protect the soul of man from destruction by the soulless machine.

It can defend the spirit of individualism. It must champion the human soul in its God-given right to exercise freely the faculties of mind and body. We must defend the right to work against those who would either destroy or degrade it. We must defend the right of every man, not only to join with others in protecting his interests, whether he is a brain worker or a hand worker—for without the right of combination the individual would often be the victim of giant forces—but we must vindicate the equal right of an individual, if he so wills, to depend upon his own strength.

The tendency of group morality to standardize man—and thus reduce all men to the dead level of an average mediocrity—is one that the law should combat. Its protection should be given to those of superior skill and diligence, who ask the due rewards of such superiority. Any other course, to use the fine phrase of Thomas Jefferson in his first inaugural, is to "take from the mouth of labour the bread it has earned."

Of this spirit one of the noblest expressions is the Constitution of the United States. That Magna Charta has not wholly escaped the destructive tendencies of a mechanical age. It was framed at the very end of the pastoral-agricultural age and at a time when the spirit of individualism was in full flower. The hardy pioneers who, with their axes, made straight the pathway of an advancing civilization, were sturdy men who need not be undervalued to us of the mechanical age. The "prairie schooner," which met the elemental forces of Nature with the proud challenge: "Pike's Peak or bust," produced as fine a type of manhood as the age which travels either in Mr. Ford's "fliver" or the more luxurious Rolls-Royce.

The Constitution was framed in the period that marked the passing of the primitive age and the dawn of the day of the machine. Watt had recently discovered the potency of steam vapour as a motive power; but its only use at first was for pumping water out of the mines.

When the framers of the Constitution met in high convention in Philadelphia in the summer of 1787, a Connecticut Yankee, John Fitch, was then also working in Philadelphia upon his steamboat; but twenty years were to pass before the prow of the Clermont was to part the waters of the Hudson, and nearly a half century before transportation was to be revolutionized by the utilization of Watt's invention in the locomotive. Of the wonders of the steamship, the railroad, the telegraphic cable, the wireless, the gasoline engine, and a thousand other mechanical miracles, the framers of the American Constitution did not even dream.

The greatest and noblest purpose of the Constitution was not alone to hold in nicest equipose the relative powers of the nation and the States, but also to maintain in the scales of justice a true equilibrium between the rights of government and the rights of an individual. It did not believe that the State was omnipotent or infallible, and yet it proclaimed its authority within wise and just limits. It defended the integrity of the human soul.

In other governments, these fundamental decencies of liberty rest upon the conscience of the legislature. Under the American Constitution, they are part of the fundamental law, and, as such, enforceable by judges sworn to defend the integrity of the individual as fully as the integrity of the State.

When did a nobler "vision" inspire men in the political annals of mankind? Without that vision to restrain each succeeding generation of Americans from the tempting excesses of political power, the American Commonwealth, with its great heterogeneous democracy, would probably perish.

That vision still remains as an ideal with the American people and still leads them to ever-higher achievements, for in all the mad changes of a frenzied hour, they have not yet lost faith in or love for the Constitution of the Fathers! That vision will remain with them as long, and no longer, as there is in their hearts a conscious and willing acquiescence in its wisdom and justice. Obviously, it can have no inherent vigour to perpetuate itself. If it ceases to be of the spirit of the people, then the yellow parchment whereon it is inscribed can avail nothing. When that parchment was last taken from the safe in the State Department, the ink in which it had been engrossed nearly 134 years ago was found to have faded. All who believe in constitutional government must hope that this is not a portentous symbol. The American people must write the compact, not with ink upon parchment, but with "letters of living light"—to use Webster's phrase—upon their hearts.

Again the solemn warning of the wise man of old recurs to us:

"Where there is no vision, the people perish; but he that keepeth the law, happy is he."